$HOT DOWN!

$HOT DOWN!

CAPITAL CRIMES
OF CASPER, WYOMING

CHARLOTTE BABCOCK

HIGH PLAINS PRESS

FIRST PRINTING

10 9 8 7 6 5 4 3 2 1

*The cover photograph on the trade paperback
edition shows Casper at night in about 1910.*
(Courtesy Casper College Library)

*The cover illustration on the trade paperback
edition is an adaptation of Frederic Remington's "A
Row in a Cattle Town."*

Library of Congress Cataloging-in-Publication Data

Babcock, Charlotte
Shot down! : capital crimes of Casper, Wyoming /
by Charlotte Babcock.
        p.   cm.
ISBN 0-931271-51-7 (cloth)
ISBN 0-931271-52-5 (trade paper)
1. Murder--Wyoming--Casper--History.
2. Criminal justice, Administration of--
Wyoming--Casper--History.
I. Title.
HV6534.C29B33   1999
364.15'23'0978793--dc21   99-25763
CIP

HIGH PLAINS PRESS
539 CASSA ROAD
GLENDO, WYOMING 82213
ORDERS: 1-800-552-7819

CONTENTS

FOREWORD

INCE I FIRST LEARNED that Charlotte Babcock was writing a book about the crimes that occurred in early-day Casper, Wyoming, I have eagerly awaited the results. Along with many others, I am a fan of her work, and knew that this new book would be peppered with original insights and witticisms.

These stories are told as if by the drawing-room fireplace of someone who was there, a neighbor who was thoroughly conversant with the facts and could get the whole story straight for those of us who were out of town when the events transpired. Recounted here are the crimes, chases, and courtroom dramas that captivated the citizens of Casper in its early days, stories of scandal and wickedness that brought standing-room-only crowds to the courthouses and drew lynch mobs into the streets crying for justice.

Sensational in their own right, these events have been thoroughly researched by the author and are accurately reported, insofar as the available facts allow.

The fabric of history is made up of such stories of the past. The events that transpired, as well as the reactions of those who participated in them or witnessed their aftermath, are a window to the past—our past. Take a look then, through this window, and watch those events unfold before your eyes as you read this wonderful book. It will be a load of fun.

KEVIN S. ANDERSON, WESTERN HISTORY SPECIALIST,

CASPER COLLEGE GOODSTEIN FOUNDATION LIBRARY

PREFACE

WHEN I STARTED TO explore the colorful criminal history of Casper, Wyoming, simply as an interesting "pastime" for a native Casperite, I had no intention of getting *really* involved. But before I knew it, I was hooked.

I'd heard and read many of the stories about Casper's wild, sometimes lurid, frontier days: the murders, the hanging, the beautiful and bad dance hall queen, the adulteries, and all the rest. I quickly discovered that Casper's past had been written about in all manner of publications—and by a number of historians—with astounding variety. Drawing all these accounts together and sifting through them became an intriguing exercise in dogged detection, and in some measure, interpretation. I came to realize that many times the telling of a particular drama did, indeed, depend upon the interpretation of the writer. Actual eyewitness accounts of certain actions or events tended to vary and, in some cases, contradict each other to the extent that, once in a while, no clear conclusion could be reached.

The further I delved into these inconsistencies the more I felt compelled to solve them. Sometimes I felt that I had succeeded and sometimes, as I combed through the details of a legend, I knew I hadn't—and the mystery of the tale would remain just that. Brigham D. Madsen, the esteemed historian, succeeded in bringing my dilemma into focus for me with his words about the role of historian as a truth-teller. He wrote, "What is truth? What really happened? That's why historians are not liked sometimes, because we destroy myths."

In bringing together some of my favorite early-day stories I hope I have not destroyed any of them except in the name of accuracy. It is possible that, in spite of my desire to get to the bottom of each story and do it justice, I may have made a mistake or two myself, though I would hang my head in shame were it so.

While I wrote this volume I drew heavily on period newspapers, court transcripts, and numerous valuable books of Wyoming history. When I quoted from newspapers I retained all the colorful original misspellings, errors, and idiosyncrasies as they appeared in print. Readers who are unfamiliar with Wyoming history should know that Alfred J. Mokler was a proficient chronicler of its early history in his role as newspaper writer, editor and publisher, and prolific author, whose many writings were invaluable to me.

ACKNOWLEDGEMENTS

MANY AND SINCERE thanks are due to a number of people without whose encouragement and help I would probably not have finished this book.

To my husband, Robert, who did so much in finding sources and recording data to keep me going but, most of all, in operating a computer whose intricacies still manage to defeat my best efforts. He did manage to teach me some few rudimentary skills, though at great peril to his sanity.

To Kevin Anderson, talented and knowledgeable archivist and Western History Specialist at Casper College who, no matter how busy, was always ready and able to dig up the most obscure document or photograph and talk things over with me.

To Lee Underbrink, historian and friend, who could answer—or find the answer to—any question I asked him.

To Scott Homar in Cheyenne for his help in the Hurt story.

To the Natrona County Library's librarians Patty Patterson and Lida Volin, who were always gracious and accommodating in helping me with the microfiche.

To the late Donna Davis, Casper College photographer, for her many photographic skills. Donna passed away at age fifty-seven, before she could see the completion of this book.

To Mindy Keskinen, editor extraordinaire, who was a joy to work with. And to Nancy Curtis, publisher, High Plains Press, at whose insistence I wrote this book, for her infinite patience in waiting me out.

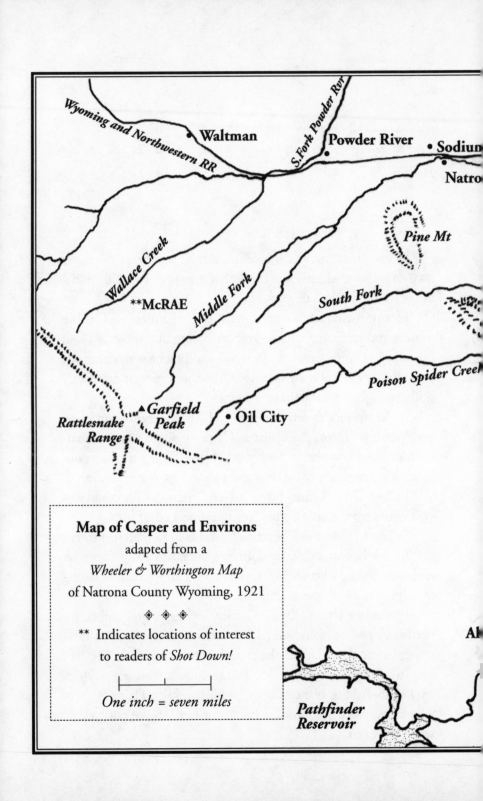

Map of Casper and Environs

adapted from a

Wheeler & Worthington Map

of Natrona County Wyoming, 1921

❖ ❖ ❖

** Indicates locations of interest
to readers of *Shot Down!*

One inch = seven miles

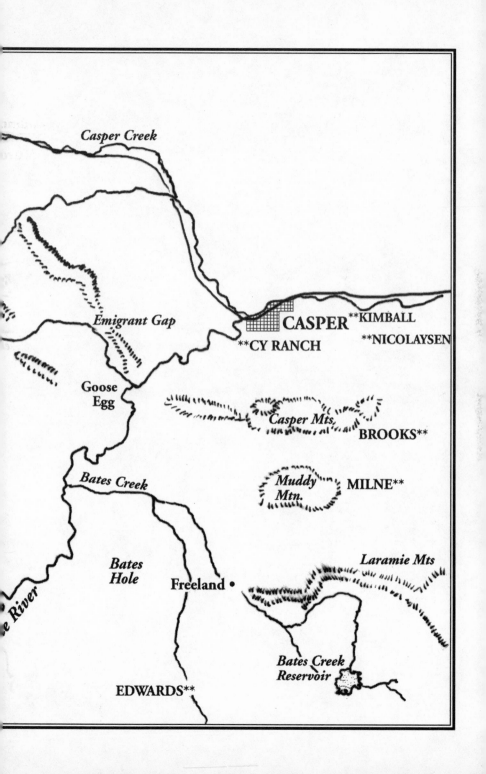

CHAPTER ONE

CASPER'S FIRST MURDER

ALTHOUGH THE WINDSWEPT prairie town of Casper, Wyoming, was just over a year old in 1890 and harbored only 544 people, it boasted a railroad, the Fremont, Elkhorn and Missouri Valley; the Park Hotel; a newspaper, the *Casper Weekly Mail;* and at least a half-dozen saloons. These drinking establishments were strictly relegated to the west side of Center Street between Second Street and Midwest Avenue—except for one. That special saloon was located on South Wolcott Street on the site of the present-day city parking facility. Why it was allowed this special location is a matter for conjecture, but it was whispered about that it enjoyed the privilege of having very influential friends and/or backers. The establishment was called the Dance House, and it was the source of two tragic events in the rowdy, wide-open town of Casper.

The Dance House was run by a creepy, short (five-foot-four), mean-tempered character named Black Dogae Lee—the "Black" probably referred to his beady, close-set black eyes and his dark, droopy mustache. At the saloon the customers could partake of a selection of dance hall "girls," in addition to gambling and dancing. The girls' quarters consisted of four little houses out back for liaisons, if patrons were so inclined. A musician named H.J. "Sonny" Summers, Jr., played violin and piano. Customers called him the "Ragtime Kid." The Dance House was a popular place.

13

The star attraction at the Dance House, however, was the beautiful twenty-three-year-old Louella Polk, who was Black Dogae's partner, business and otherwise. She had a multitude of admirers, but she was also known to be Black Dogae's private property, and he was extremely jealous of the attention paid to her by other men. His jealousy became a consuming passion which finally got the better of him one day in May 1890, when he tricked the lovely Lou into joining him on a ride that would change her life forever.

Mary Helen Hendry's in-depth chronicle of Lou Polk, *Petticoats & Pistols*, notes that Lou was an accomplished rider, and that after she and Dogae had ridden east out of Casper and crossed the Platte River, Black Dogae had worked himself into a rage, began to rant, and threatened Lou with bodily harm and even death. Lou became very frightened. When they happened to meet a herder driving a team she tried to enlist his help, but Dogae threatened to kill her on the spot if she didn't stay with him. The herder reported the meeting to Sheriff W. W. Jaycox in Casper—but not until the next day.

The sheriff immediately set out to locate the pair, but his search proved fruitless. At one point he came within a few hundred yards of them, although he didn't know it. Lou saw him, she recounted later, but Black Dogae held her down in a gulch with his gun pressed to her head.

At last, mad and desperate after dragging Lou all over the countryside for days with virtually no food or water, Dogae ended up at a ranch house somewhere near Wendover, about one hundred miles southeast of Casper. After running off the ranch man by threatening to shoot and kill him, he dragged Lou into the house, threw her down and, in a violent burst, brutally cut off her nose. Then he helped himself to the rancher's Winchester, jumped on the rancher's fresh horse, and rode away.

When the rancher returned to the house, he found the horribly mutilated Lou. He gathered her up and took her to Wendover.

The Wyoming Derrick Building stood on the west side of Center Street not far from the Graham House. Pictured from left: Uncle Matt Campfield, double amputee Civil War veteran and first elected coroner of Casper, sits on hitching rail; standing by the door of the Derrick *are John "Posthole" McGrath, W.S. Kimball, and Laura Stroud, who later married McGrath. Two unidentified men stand farther right, and Dad Eads sits right on the hitching rail.* (Frances Seely Webb Collection: courtesy Casper College Library)

Lou carried along her severed nose, which she had wrapped in a wet handkerchief. But no one in Wendover could do anything for her, so she rode on to Douglas in the mail carrier's wagon—another futile trip because the doctor there couldn't mend her damaged face, either.

However, Lou's mother, a lady by the name of Armilla Mason, lived in Douglas, and Lou stayed there with her for several days. Then the two of them returned to Casper where Lou's horrible experience was reported, in her own words, in the first issue of the new *Wyoming Derrick* newspaper, dated May 21, 1890, under the headline, "A Devil's Deed."

We started out, as I supposed, for a pleasure ride and visit to Tom Hood's sheep camp, but from the time we were seen by the sheepherder after we crossed the bridge near Casper, I was an unwilling prisoner. Dogae forced me to accompany him by means of all kinds of horrible threats and a six-shooter. Sometimes he said he would kill me, and again that he was going to take me to Kansas. We rode without food for two days, when Dogae killed a rabbit, and I ate part of it raw in a cabin near Fetterman. Then we went without a morsel of food for four whole days, traveling nights and hiding in the bushes along the streams during the day. Finally, on the day he cut my nose off, we were hid in a gulch when I happened to raise my head and saw Sheriff Jaycox passing a few hundred yards away. Dogae saw him at the same time, and pulling me to the ground placed his six-shooter to my ear and said if I moved he would blow my brains out. That same day we went to the cow camp. The boys told Dogae he had better turn back and give himself up. Dogae said he would, but as soon as the boys went away he made the ranchman leave and told me he was going to cut my nose off and gouge out one of my eyes. He held me on the floor and cut my nose off, as you can see, but did not touch my eyes. Then he got on a horse and rode away.

The search for Black Dogae Lee began in earnest, but to no avail. He disappeared without a trace and was never seen or heard of again.

Louella's terrible ordeal gained her much sympathy in Casper—but just temporarily. She apparently decided she was not going to let her terrible disfigurement get in the way of what she felt she had coming to her. (She sometimes hid her face with veils, spectacles, or a wax nose. Sometimes she didn't.) She became a bitter, cynical person—and who could blame her?

That summer, Lou bought out the Dance House from the property owners for $175 and the fun began. There was prostitution, gambling, fights, loud music—the works—and it went on day and night, *all* night. The goings-on seemed to be uncontrollable and the town's law enforcement just looked the other way. The ex-lovely Lou was raking in money and becoming bolder about it by the day. She didn't seem to care what anyone thought.

Around September 20 (reports conflict on the date), Lou bought a pistol and gave it to her bartender-bouncer, a rather notorious gunman named John Conaway. (The spelling "Conaway" soon became "Conway" in written reports. The first spelling was used because the gunman claimed he was the nephew of Judge Asbury B. Conaway, who had been elected chief justice of the Wyoming Supreme Court. His claim was never substantiated and the spelling of his name settled on "Conway.") Lou let it be known that she supplied him the gun to restore law and order in her establishment.

A widely honored literary maxim states that if a gun appears on the scene, it has to go off. And that is just what happened with Lou's gun on Saturday evening, September 20: a tragedy that became Casper's first murder. The *Wyoming Derrick* reported on September 25 under screaming banner headlines:

MURDER!

ALMOST A LYNCHING!

BARTENDER JOHN CONAWAY MURDERS COWBOY A.J. TIDWELL!

**An Excuseless Murder Committed in Cold Blood in a
Casper Dance House Kept by the Notorious Lou Polk.
One Person Has an Eye Gouged Out.
Cowboys Indignant Over the Murder of Their Comrade.
Would Have Lynched the Murderer,
Had Not the Officers Secreted Him.
Attempted to Burn the Dance House.**

Looking north on Center Street, 1890. The hotel is the Graham House which was located on the northwest corner of present-day Midwest and Center Streets, where the Employment Security Building now stands. By 1900 the Graham House had become the Warner House. (Frances Seely Webb Collection: courtesy Casper College Library)

The first murder, and like-wise the first death in Casper, occurred on Saturday night of last week [September 20] at about eleven o'clock in the dance house conducted by the notorious Lou Polk at which time and place John Conaway shot and almost instantly killed A.J. Tidwell, better known as "Red Jack", a cowboy in the employ of the FL cattle company.

A number of cowboys were in town the evening in question, and as is their wont when in town, visited the dance house for A LITTLE LARK and "Red Jack" was among their number.

H.J. Summers, Jr., better known as "Sonny", a violinist, was chief musician at the hall that evening and along about eleven o'clock, when the boys had begun to feel the effects of their numerous drinks, Jimmie Hines, one of the cowboys, approached "Sonny", with whom he was acquainted, and saluted him familiarly. "Sonny" was not feeling well and failed to respond, whereupon Hines became indignant and picked a quarrel. [Hines testified later that he remarked to those around him, "Let's make the son of a bitch speak."] The matter was finally peacefully settled but a little later Hines conceived the idea of renewing the quarrel and solicited the assistance of "Red Jack." As soon as the quarrel was renewed, Conaway, who was acting as barkeeper, took a hand, and he and "Red Jack" exchanged a few blows. But Conaway suddenly broke away, and running back of the bar grabbed up a six-shooter and began flourishing it. None of the cowboys were armed, having deposited their six-shooters with friends, to prevent the possibility of bloodshed, as was their custom before starting in on a spree. Consequently, there was a general stampede when Conaway began flourishing his gun. Nearly everybody ran out at the north door, including "Sonny", who ran against a limb of a pine tree standing in front of the door and GOUGED HIS LEFT EYE OUT.

The now-dead pine tree had been lashed to a post there since the Fourth of July celebration. Casper itself, though it lay between Casper Mountain on the south and the North Platte River on the north, was bereft of trees except for the cottonwoods along the river bank. The flat, wind-blown terrain, however, didn't lack sand, sagebrush, or cactus. So, in order to make the town appear somewhat green and festive for special occasions, it was the custom for residents to cut down pine trees on Casper Mountain and haul them to town for decoration. This particular tree, at least, had never been removed. The *Derrick's* report continued:

"Red Jack" ran out of the east door [the door which faced Wolcott Street] with Conaway in close pursuit. When he saw Conaway coming out at the door he exclaimed, "I am going! I am going!" But Conaway paid no attention and rushing up to him struck him on the head with his six-shooter and knocked him down. After which he DELIBERATELY SHOT HIM as he lay upon the ground.

The bullet pierced Tidwell's left side, severed the femoral artery, and exited on his left side just above the hip. He probably died instantly.

One of the dance hall girls ran to get Constable Patton who was in his own saloon—probably over on Center Street. Patton had heard the shot and had his own gun in hand when the girl arrived. According to the paper she said, "Oh, come quick. They are fighting and shooting over at the dance hall."

When Patton got there, Conaway met him and said, "Well, I guess I am your prisoner. Here's my gun."

Patton asked him what he had done and he said, "I knocked a lame fellow down and shot at him."

Apparently puzzled, the *Derrick's* reporter made this aside: "It is not known why he said this, as Jack was not lame, but on the contrary a large, powerful and well built man."

Patton ordered Conaway to come with him over to his saloon, but Conaway didn't want to go without his own gun: he thought Tidwell's friends would probably try to shoot him. Patton eventually got him there, put a guard on him, and went back to the Dance House to see what he could do. Tidwell had been carried into the building and was dead.

Conaway was then put in jail under guard because the outraged cowboys were already threatening to lynch him.

At an inquest held the next morning it was determined that "Tidwell came to his death by a shot fired from a pistol in the hands of John Conaway without just cause of provocation."

The cowboys rode all over the area spreading the news of the murder and by that evening practically every "puncher" within miles had come to town to help lynch John Conaway.

Sheriff W.W. Jaycox, who had just been re-elected to his position in Natrona County's second election on September 11, decided something had to be done, so he went looking for the railroad conductor. Swearing him to secrecy, Jaycox obtained from him the key to a passenger coach standing near the railroad's engine house. The wily sheriff then delayed Tidwell's funeral until dark—making sure he, himself, was prominently in attendance. Since the cemetery was half a mile east of town (close to the Nagel Buick agency of recent times), the sheriff's officers could spirit Conaway from the jail to the train coach and hide him there with no one the wiser.

Jaycox's plan worked like a charm. The would-be cowboy lynchers returned from the funeral, guns on their hips, ready to do away with Conaway—who was not to be found. After spending the night milling around in frustration, the cowboys left town.

Conaway's preliminary hearing was held the next day. Waiving extradition, he was put on the train to Douglas where he was kept in the Converse County jail.

The newspaper reported that after the clerk read the indictment of first-degree murder to Conaway, Judge Blake said to him, "Mr. Conaway, you have heard the reading of the indictment, are you guilty or not guilty?"

Conaway replied quickly. "Not guilty."

Two days later, on Wednesday evening, September 24, a party or parties unknown tried to burn down the Dance House by pouring kerosene over the front door and floor and putting a match to it. One of the employees came along just in time to extinguish the fire before any major damage occurred. The *Derrick's* observation after the incident was that Casper citizens felt that surely a more successful attempt would soon be made at destroying this most unwanted sore in their midst. The next day it carried the following editorial:

> The *Derrick* does not in the least object to bawdy houses, nor even to dance houses, or to the class of people who inhabit the same, realizing as we do that they are in a

This structure was originally Lou Polk's dance hall. It stood on the 200 block of South Wolcott Street across the alley behind the recently-closed Kline's dress shop (Kline's was at 147 East Second). Before it was torn down in 1960, it had housed several families and a tailor shop at various times. The city's municipal parking garage stands there today. (Frances Seely Webb Collection: courtesy Casper College Library)

measure a necessity in this Western country (to insure the safety of respectable women), but Mrs. Lou Polk is a nuisance that should be abated. Even the sporting element must agree with us in this opinion, for a few more "breaks" like she has made might result in all people of that class being excluded from town—a state of affairs that we should dislike to see.

Saturday night's tragedy should prove a warning. Human life must be protected, at any cost. Jack Tidwell was killed just out of pure cussedness, by a man of whom it had been boasted was a "man killer", and who evidently wanted to show his mistress, the dance house queen, that she had not over estimated him. If we must have a dance house let it pass into the hands of someone who will at least keep an orderly place.

The editorial went on to discuss Conaway's crime and his contention that he expected leniency because of his relationship to Supreme Court Justice A.B. Conaway [which later proved unfounded]. It ended with this accusation and verdict: "His crime was murder, pure and simple, and can in no manner be considered manslaughter. It is a capital and not a penitentiary offense. Conaway should stretch hemp."

Lou Polk was incensed by these editorials, written by *Derrick* editor W.S. Kimball. Accompanied by her mother, Armilla Mason, she paid editor Kimball an unfriendly visit and threatened him with bodily harm if he didn't retract his words— which, of course, he refused to do.

Now Lou apparently decided she'd had enough of Casper. After a stay in Douglas where her mother lived, she ended up in Nevada (although some reports had her going to Idaho), where she took up residence. The Dance House was eventually sold, perhaps to cover taxes due.

John Conaway, now Conway, languished in the Douglas jail for almost a year before his trial began in Casper in September 1891. A change of venue had been denied. Conway sobbed pathetically through most of his trial and ultimately pled guilty to second-degree murder. The prosecuting attorney was Alex T. Butler. Conway was sentenced to twenty-five years at the territorial prison in Laramie. Wyoming's then-governor, John Osborne, reduced his sentence to seven years beginning August 8, 1891, and the next governor, William Richards, pardoned Conway on October 31, 1897, after he had served only six years of his sentence. After he was freed, Conway went to Colorado and back to a life of crime: he was twice sent to the penitentiary in Cañon City.

This cryptic footnote to the case appeared in the *Derrick* on September 10, 1891, two days after the trial ended:

> The Conway case has been tried and the defendant sentenced. After listening to all the evidence at the case we are inclined to believe that among the party who went over to that hall that night and started the disturbance, some at least are open to censure. The two parties who suffered most severely—Red Jack in giving up his life and Conway by living death—was not in any way interested in the quarrel when it began. Red Jack interfered to help a friend while Conway tried to preserve the peace in the house in which he was employed. Thus the fight was transferred to these two parties with a most tragic result while the real parties to blame escaped uninjured. There is a moral to this story which we will let our readers draw.

It seems logical that the editorial referred to Jimmie Hines, the cowboy who started the quarrel, and to Lou Polk, who supplied Conway with the gun.

The *Natrona Tribune* newspaper, which began publishing in June 1891, accorded John Conway a more sympathetic persona than did the *Derrick*. On September 9, 1891, the *Tribune* reported on the presence of Conway's sister and his niece at the trial. They had traveled to Casper from their home in Denver to offer him their support. The *Tribune* reporter thought the sister, Mrs. Bowman, "looked quite pleasant and the tired worn face she wore when she left the court room [the night before, September 8] had disappeared. The little girl looked jolly and one could readily see that the little one did not apprehend the trouble which seemed to be upon the mother's mind. Mrs. Bowman sat down at the end of the table and Conway immediately drew his chair close to hers. The true love and affection which exists between a brother and sister have been plainly shown here during the trial."

The *Tribune's* companion column, entitled "A Tragic End," expanded the pathos and reported that Mrs. Bowman's expression

The Fremont, Elkhorn & Missouri Valley Railroad train leaving Casper in about 1895. Art Randall states in his book, Casper "Old Town" and Fremont, Elkhorn & Missouri Valley Railroad, *that the FE & MV was consolidated into the Chicago & North Western Railroad in 1903.* (Sheffner-McFadden Collection: courtesy Casper College Library)

after the trial was not "the pleasant bright face that occurred in court" the day before, but was now "tired" and "weary."

Conway's appearance, the paper said, was "worn and troubled" and he had been "weeping." Conway's attorneys at that juncture told the court that the defendant was changing his not-guilty plea to a plea of guilty of murder in the second degree. At that, Conway's head fell and "his sobs were low and piteous."

The court accepted the change of plea and Conway was taken back to the jail, where his sister met him. They wept in each other's arms, after which the sister left, "being urged by others to go away for a little while that he [Conway] might regain himself...she went to the river bank and sat under a tree," in the *Tribune's* words.

Later that same afternoon the enterprising *Tribune* reporter went back to the jail and was allowed to see Conway. The writer asked, "Mr. Conway, do you want to talk for a while?"

"Well," Conway said, "it depends upon the nature of the conversation."

"Mr. Conway," said the reporter, "as you have not had a chance to show your side of the case in court, I have come to ask you if you would want any thing said in the paper."

Well, yes, I do, said Conway. You may state that my shooting Mr. Tidwell was an accident. I did not intend to. I did not know that he was dead for over thirty minutes afterwards. Previous to coming here I was employed as brakeman and conductor on the U.P.R.R., on which road I have worked for about 10 years, in the capacity of freight brakeman, freight conductor, and passenger conductor, out of Rawlins, Cheyenne and Denver. I run a passenger train from Denver down in Kansas for nearly two years. When I came to Casper I had my arm crushed, the accident having happened in a wreck at Rawlins about the last of August 1890. I was thinking of going to Denver to visit relatives there. I knew Lou Polk, knew her father and mother well. We lived near together in Cheyenne. When I got hurt I took a leave of absence and Lou wrote to me to come to Casper. At that time I did not know Lu's [sic] reputation, did not know she had her nose cut off, nor did I know she was running a dance house. I supposed she was as when I last heard from her. I was quite intimate with her from 1883 to 1885 when I left Central Wyoming and went to Central America. I had not heard from her from that time until August 1890 when she wanted me to come up here. When I got here I could not use my arm and had to have my meat cut up at the hotel. I intended to stay here until my arm got well.

Just as my arm had gotten better there was a rush over at the dance house and I tended bar for them at odd times. This trouble happened on Saturday night and I was going away on Monday's train and spoke to [the] drayman to haul my trunk down.

❧ ❧ ❧

Louella Polk ultimately returned to Casper about June 1907, and she returned a sick woman. She moved in with her mother, Armilla, who had divorced John Mason and married prominent Douglas saloon keeper D.A. Robertson. The couple had moved to Casper in 1893, Hendry writes, where they opened a new saloon on the west side of Center Street between Second Street and Midwest Avenue. Robertson was a respected citizen, active in the Masons, who was elected to represent Natrona County in the Wyoming legislature in 1903. The Robertsons cared for Louella after her return to Casper until she died of consumption two months later on August 16, 1907. She was forty years old. She is buried at Highland Cemetery beneath an ornate tombstone inscribed "Cocoran," above which is only her first name, Lulu, and the dates 1867–1907.

Presumably Lou had married a man named Cocoran during the years she was away from Casper. According to Hendry, she'd had at least two earlier marriages: to Estes Polk in Fort Laramie in 1886, and before that, apparently, to a Mr. White.

"Red Jack" Tidwell is also buried at Highland Cemetery, but in an unmarked grave. His remains were transferred there from the original cemetery (along with about twenty-five others) when the new Highland Cemetery was established a few years after his murder.

CHAPTER TWO

A SUNDAY TRAGEDY

CASPER HAD BARELY digested the Polk/Tidwell/Conway fracas when the next shooting occurred at about four o'clock on Sunday afternoon, May 10, 1891. This new tragedy was generally considered to be one of the saddest events in Casper's short history.

On that fateful day, the city marshal, a man by the name of Bill Hodge, shot and killed thirty-seven-year-old William Warren, a cowboy who was employed at the CY ranch just west of Casper. One of the largest cattle companies in Wyoming, if not the largest, the CY was owned by "J.M. Carey & Brother." Warren had been working at the ranch just about a month, having moved to Casper from his home in Laramie City, where his parents lived. William's brother, Joseph, was also a cowboy at the CY spread and may have helped William get his job there.

A number of the CY cowboys had ridden into town from the ranch and headed for their favorite watering hole, Crow's Saloon (situated on the west side of Center Street, between Second and Midwest Streets), where Warren, at least, proceeded to get roaring drunk and aggressive while playing stud poker. After a while, feeling he needed a larger arena than the saloon offered, Warren went out into the street and began to proclaim to the bystanders that he was ready to fight and that he could lick any goddamned son-of-a-bitch that ever walked—

sentiments that were not appreciated by the many people who were walking home from their Sunday School classes which had just been dismissed.

Someone went to find Marshal Hodge, who was visiting with friends in the parlor of the Graham House hotel on the southwest corner of Midwest and Center Streets. By the time Hodge arrived on the scene, Warren had gone back into the saloon.

Now some uncertainties enter the story. A spectator, Mr. P.A. Demorest, said that he saw the marshal come along the street, look into the saloon, and walk on. The marshal apparently went around to the back door of Crow's Saloon and entered from there. However, A.J. Mokler's *History of Natrona County* relates that the marshal told Warren, there in the street, to get back inside the saloon and not to come out again or he would arrest him.

Inside the saloon, Warren's cowboy buddies were trying to get him out the door, onto his horse, and out of town. But as soon as Warren mounted his horse, he commenced whipping and spurring it and, of course, the horse began to buck and pitch wildly. It bucked across the street and onto the sidewalk, nearly smashing through the front of the Winslow store. Warren's hat fell off, and one of his friends picked it up and gave it to him. He put it on and spurred his horse again.

Marshal Hodge came out the front door of the saloon and started across the street with his hand on his gun. One of the bystanders heard him say that he was going to "run him in."

Warren was not armed.

At this point, reports of the scene begin to vary seriously. Some witnesses claimed the marshal said something to Warren. Others said he didn't. Then Hodge fired his Colt .45; accounts conflict about whether he fired at Warren or into the air.

Warren's horse began to gallop. Warren dropped the reins, but not the hackamore rope which was wrapped around his arm. He swung the rope, first to one side of the horse and then to the other. The horse spooked.

"Old Town" Casper, 1888. In the summer of 1888 "Old Town" was established approximately where East Yellowstone and North McKinley Streets intersect now. A new downtown Casper was platted that fall and many buildings were soon moved to Second and Center Streets. The Demorest Home Restaurant is the second false-fronted building from the left. (Sheffner-McFadden Collection: courtesy Casper College Library)

Hodge fired again.

Warren's horse bucked two or three times and Warren fell off, fatally wounded.

The postmortem examination showed that Hodge's second bullet had entered Warren's body five inches to the right of his spine and grazed a vertebra, where it was deflected and passed through the abdomen, killing him instantly.

Warren's friends, the CY cowboys, were horrified and very angry at what they felt was a totally unwarranted shooting. They were eager to go after Hodge and lynch him.

Hodge's friends were able to hide him in another saloon up the block until the angry cowboys could be somewhat calmed down. Meanwhile the cowboys wasted no time in filing a complaint demanding that Hodge be arrested at once.

Hodge agreed to surrender to Lew Seely, a prominent citizen whose store was in the same block. Seely remarked that while he could not understand why Hodge had shot Warren, "we have made him our marshal and it is our duty to stand behind him and give him our full support; we can't let the cowboys lynch him and shoot up the town."

His remarks were not taken kindly by Warren's friends.

Frances Seely Webb, Lew Seely's daughter and a noted authority on Casper history, quoted Hodge in the *Casper Chronicles* as saying that "Warren always became quarrelsome when drinking." She also described Hodge's surrender to Seely: "Hodge was taken out the back way to a saloon building up the block, which was easy to defend, and several friends of Hodge and men who meant to defend the town from a lawless element, barricaded themselves in the building with Hodge. Finding it impossible to get at Hodge, the cowboys asked that he be arrested. Hodge said that he would surrender to one man only—Lew Seely." That was, Mrs. Webb explained, due to her father's earlier remarks.

Seely was duly sworn in as marshal and Hodge surrendered to him.

Casper's opinions were almost evenly divided about whether Hodge was justified in shooting Warren. The *Wyoming Derrick* had this to say:

> Sentiment is…divided upon the shooting. While all admit that the action of the marshal was hasty, rash and unjustifiable, that he exceeded his authority and permitted the time to pass when he ought properly to have made the arrest, many think that he should be in a measure upheld, as a lesson to persons who might in the future be inclined to attempt to run the town. Cowboys were angry almost to desperation, and it would have required but a spark to explode the magazine that hung over the head of Marshal Hodge and even endangered the town. However by the

advice of the cooler and older heads in their ranks, the boys, though feeling greatly injured and grossly outraged, as they were, wisely concluded to not make matters worse in which decision they displayed more sense and better judgement than a like number of citizens would be likely to have done. One seldom sees a more intelligent and gentlemanly set of boys than in the employ of the CY, and their course throughout is certainly to be highly commended. It has certainly made them many friends...

The shooting of Wm. Warren by Wm. Hodge is certainly the saddest event that has transpired in the history of Casper—one long to be remembered, deeply regretted and deplored.

The young Warren's funeral was held on Tuesday evening, May 12, after his grieving parents and his two other brothers could get to Casper. A large number of Casperites attended his service to express their sympathies to the family.

Bill Hodge was bound over and stood trial on September 4, 1891, in the district court, immediately following John Conway's trial. The *Derrick* printed Hodge's verbatim account of the shooting. No mention was made of the exact charges brought against him.

Am defendant in the action. On May 10 last was town marshal of Casper. On the afternoon of that day was at Graham House, just prior to death of Warren ...Mr. Graham called me out saying a man was using bad language on the streets. Got my hat and went to Crow's saloon. Came right out and saw Warren there but didn't know him. In about five minutes I came back from being up the street and saw Nicholson [a man inside Crow's saloon]. I asked if that [referring to Warren] was a CY man and told him [Nicholson] to take him home; went back to water closet in Crow's saloon after [I] saw Warren get on his horse. I was there in saloon, Warren was cursing and talking about good riding; I saw him spur his horse and whip him with rope; his horse bucked and Warren lost his hat and had no trouble stopping his horse to get it. One of the boys handed it to him and he spurred his horse and bucked over to Winslow's. I came out of Crow's saloon when the horse got on the sidewalk and I started out on a run. I put my hand on my pistol to hold it down. I told Warren to stop and he said, "yes I will like hell." I then pulled my gun and held it down under the horse and shot. I was simply shooting to scare him and make him stop; he went on and I again called to him to stop. I then threw my gun down toward the ground and shot. I had no intention of shooting. I didn't go out soon-er and arrest him because he wasn't doing anything inside building; he was disturbing peace. He was making the horse buck and it was likely to jump on a lady or child; Sunday school was letting out and he was endangering lives of others. I was the first man to him, he called my name and said, "I'll let up, Hodge." I called Dr. Benson to come to the man and I said, "I think he is badly hurt from his fall." Benson said he was not shot.

The first time I knew he was shot was in about an hour when some one told me he was dead.

The next day Hodge was subjected to an intense cross-ex-amination which caused him to garble his story considerably. The case was then given to the jury in the late afternoon.

The jury deliberated until about eleven o'clock that night but couldn't reach a consensus, so they began again the next morning. By three-thirty that afternoon—after hours of deliber-ation—they gave it up and informed the court that they could not come to a decision. (The rumor was that the jury panel stood eleven to one for a conviction.) They were discharged, the case was continued until the next term of the district court, and Hodge's bond was fixed at three thousand dollars.

William Hodge was ultimately acquitted after his second trial, when evidence was presented indicating that the bullet that killed William Warren had ricocheted off a stone in the street before it hit the young cowboy.

The *Wyoming Derrick* of November 12, 1891, reported that town marshal Lew Seely had resigned, and Tom McGrath was appointed to serve the unexpired term. Lew Seely was a most reluctant marshal, but had agreed to stay on in the position just until the Hodge case was resolved, even though there were threats against his life during Hodge's trial. However Mokler's *History of Natrona County* states that Seely resigned on June 10, 1891, exactly one month after the Sunday shooting and, according to Frances Webb's account, "much to his wife's relief."

Nearly forty years later, the *Casper Tribune-Herald* carried this obituary on April 6, 1930, notable for what it omits. "Funeral services for William Hodge, 77, who dropped dead in his room at the bunk house of the Midwest Refinery Friday night will be held at 2:30 this afternoon from the Elks home under the direction of the Muck Funeral Home.

"Mr. Hodge, a pioneer resident of Natrona County for 50 years, and a one-time peace officer of Casper, was one of the oldest employees of the Midwest Refining Company, beginning 19 years ago. He was born February 27, 1853. He was at Buffalo before coming here. He is a member of the Elks Lodge. Mr. Hodge, who is unmarried, is survived by only one sister."

CHAPTER THREE

THE MAN WHO CRIED WOLF ONCE TOO OFTEN

DOCTOR JOSEPH Benson, age fifty-one, had been a resident of Casper for only about two years when he died in the early morning hours of Sunday, October 11, 1891, the victim of his own drunken excess. He was well known throughout the surrounding country, not only as a competent and respected physician, but also as a drunk and an accomplished "storyteller," which when translated meant *liar*.

According to the *Wyoming Derrick* (October 15, 1891) Dr. Benson's true name was Joseph P. Riley, and for about fifteen years before coming to Casper he had led a truly colorful and exciting life. He had apparently served at several Western forts— Reno, Robinson, Laramie, and Steele—in a variety of roles: surgeon, nurse, scout, and overland mail carrier.

His versatility didn't end there. When he was slightly drunk, Benson liked to tell that he had been an ordained Catholic priest for twenty-one years and had been "kicked out" of the church, so to speak, because of his drinking. To give him credit, he certainly seemed to know the ritual of the Latin mass because he could be heard chanting it frequently in his room at night— drunk, of course.

When Dr. Benson was drinking—which during his final year seemed to be most of the time—he often explained why he changed his name. His romantic tale was that as a young man he had fallen deeply in love with a beautiful young lady who died shortly before they were to be married. Prostrated by grief, he promised her on her deathbed that he would be forever faithful to her memory by taking her name, since she would never live long enough to marry him and take his name.

But when he got *really* drunk, another not-so-romantic version surfaced. Benson would then confide that he had been mixed up in a fatal shooting somewhere back east, found guilty, and sentenced to fifteen years. He escaped from prison by hiding in a bread wagon and fleeing to the West under a new name— perhaps a more likely tale than the unrequited love story. The *Natrona Tribune* carried yet another version of the origins of the good doctor in its issue of June 17, 1891. (This paper was edited and published by J. Enos Waite who apologized for the lack of proofreading and the resulting errors and promised to do better as the bugs got ironed out.)

The paper reported: "Dr. Benson came to Wyoming in June 1866 from St. Joe, Mo. with a freight outfit, which was hauling supplies to Ft. Casper [Caspar] and to Camp Brown [where Lander now stands] and on through to Salt Lake City. Returning he stopped here and went north into Montana. Later he was army sargant and was stationed at Fort Laramie, Fort Russell and elsewhere. The doctor received his education at two of the best colleges in Massachusetts, one being Harvard. Massachusetts is his native state. Since coming to the west Benson has practiced nearly everywhere with good result."

It was Saturday evening, October 10, 1891, when Dr. Benson's last earthly adventure began. Drunk again, he had a fistfight with a fellow doctor named Naulteus, probably over the treatment of a patient who had been shot. Benson had decided to perform what he called a postmortem examination on the patient, "Dutch Pete" Kramhoft, even though the poor fellow was still alive. But Alex T. Butler, the prosecuting attorney in the Kramhoft shooting incident, had got wind of Benson's intention.

Dr. Joseph Benson had led a colorful and exciting life as Joseph P. Riley.
(Courtesy Natrona County Pioneer Association)

Fearing for his client's well-being, Butler immediately swore out a warrant for Benson's arrest, and the sheriff threw the doctor in jail.

Meanwhile, Dutch Pete immediately filed a malpractice suit against the doctor—and who could blame him? A postmortem on a still-living patient was something not to be taken kindly by the patient.

Dr. Benson was no stranger to the jail. He had spent many a night there sobering up and creating all the rumpus he could by yelling, "Fire! Murder! Help!" all night long, hoping that his cries would cause someone to come and let him out. He had also threatened at least once to burn down the jail the next time he was arrested.

The Casper jail was a small, square, wooden building on the west side of Center Street between Second and First Streets. It was built at a cost of three hundred dollars and had only two cells. Dr. Benson was the sole guest that night. As soon as he was locked up, he began to chant Indian war chants which gave way to imitations of wild animals, after which he began hollering, "Help! Fire! Murder!"

Granville E. Butler (he was referred to as "Justice Butler" in the paper and should not be confused with Alex T. Butler, the attorney), whose house was nearby, heard Benson but didn't pay him any mind. He did, however, take a stroll around the jail before going to bed. He thought he smelled something burning but saw no sign of a fire anywhere. A number of the other neighboring residents heard the doctor hollering, too, but they also knew how he carried on and, likewise, paid him no mind.

It was about three or four o'clock in the morning when Granville Butler's daughter, Franc, was awakened by Benson's terrible yelling. She got up and looked out her window, which faced the jail. She saw a faint flickering light and woke her father. When he went out, he saw the jail in flames, heard Benson's cries for help and immediately got a sledgehammer and tried to break the jail's lock, with no luck. He then went after

Casper's first jail stood on the west side of South Center Street between First and Second Streets, north across the alley from the present-day Cutting Board. It burned to the ground, set afire by its only prisoner, Dr. Joe Benson, who perished in the blaze on the night of October 10, 1891. (Frances Seely Webb Collection: courtesy Casper College Library)

the marshal who had the key to the jail—but the lock had been jammed by the hammering and they couldn't open it. By now a hole had burned through the south side of the building. Several men took axes and chopped a larger opening there, hoping to get Benson out, but it was too late.

The rescuers found the doctor face down on the floor, literally burned almost to ashes. They couldn't get in because of the intense heat, so they used a long rake to scoop him out. He was unrecognizable. They took his charred remains to the town hall. Since Casper had no water supply, the jail burned completely.

W.S. Kimball, a Casper pioneer, was one of the party who tried to rescue the hapless Benson. In the 1940s Mr. Kimball wrote a column for the *Casper Tribune-Herald* called "Ye Good

Old Days." His eyewitness account in a column about Benson's death said that the men's valiant efforts to extricate Benson came to naught and "We finally gave up and stood and watched it [the jail] burn down to a bed of coals that could be raked away from all there was of the mortal remains of Dr. Benson.

"His feet and ankles were consumed, as were the hands and forearms; the hair and scalp was burned from the skull, but otherwise the trunk was pretty well intact."

A coroner's jury was impaneled Sunday morning and concluded that Dr. Benson came to his death while incarcerated in jail in the town of Casper, by fire set inside the jail by his own hand. The doctor was buried Sunday evening.

The *Derrick* theorized that the doctor "called for help and the night wind bore his frantic cries to the ears of hosts of men who would have hastened to his assistance but that he had cried 'wolf' so often before no attention was paid to him." The article ended: "The doctor with all his faults had many good points. He was a man of brilliant attainments, but strong drink got the best of him and his untimely and tragic death is much to be regretted.

"He leaves a wife and child somewhere in Montana."

◈　◈　◈

The rest of the story, as radio commentator Paul Harvey might say, is that Deitleff "Dutch Pete" Kramhoft, upon whom Dr. Benson tried to perform a living postmortem, did die on the morning of November 2 at the Wentworth Hotel in Casper. He died as the result of a gunshot wound incurred when he and a ranch hand, Virgil Turner, got into a fracas in September at the B.B. Brooks ranch northeast of Casper where both of them worked. They argued over milking the cows and Dutch Pete, thirty-five years old, a large and powerful man, cursed the fourteen-year-old Turner and threatened to whip him. The frightened Turner retreated to the bunkhouse and found a .22 rifle. Dutch Pete followed him and Turner demanded that Dutch Pete take back all he'd said including the threat to whip him.

Dutch Pete refused, made a grab for the gun, and caught it by the barrel. In their struggle, the gun went off, its bullet lodging in Dutch Pete's left side.

Unfortunately, B.B. Brooks was in Cheyenne, so it fell to Mrs. Brooks and the hired lady to get Dutch Pete to Casper with the help of neighbors. The wounded Kramhoft requested the services of Dr. Benson who was on the case for about ten days. It was Benson's decision to perform the postmortem on his living patient that got him thrown in jail for the last time, October 10. On that day Kramhoft filed a malpractice suit against Benson.

A charge of attempted murder was filed against Virgil Turner on October 14 but that charge was reduced to assault and battery after a statement to the court from Dutch Pete was read. It said he himself was to blame for the shooting and that Turner should not be held responsible. Prosecuting attorney Alex Butler agreed to the reduction of charges. Young Turner was then convicted, sentenced to three months in the county jail, and served his sentence in Douglas, Wyoming, beginning October 15, 1891.

CHAPTER FOUR

THE HURT SCANDAL

A s EARLY AS March 1890 most of the Casper community knew the names Hurt and Milne, if not the families themselves. When Natrona County officially broke from Carbon County, one of the first acts of its new commissioners was to establish voting precincts and election judges. One of the appointed Casper precinct judges was Joel J. Hurt. One of the Muddy precinct judges was James Milne.

The Milne family came from Scotland and had not been in Casper very long, but then the town itself had only been incorporated the previous year. The family lived east of Casper at Walters, Wyoming, where James Milne had staked his claim. Jane and James Milne had two sons, James and William. Hardly more than a post office designation, Walters was located almost on the Converse County line at the east end of Casper Mountain.

The *Natrona Tribune* on April 15, 1894, carried the homestead application notice of James Milne's intention to make final proof, continuing his residence and the cultivation of the land under his claim. (Later, in 1902, James Milne—either father or son—would be a member of Sheriff Charles Ricker's posse when the sheriff was gunned down by Charles Woodard.)

William, the younger brother, dealt in sheep, running them "on shares" with the flocks of prominent Casper sheepman Joel J. Hurt.

The Milnes, perhaps because they did not live right in Casper, were not as socially prominent or as much written about as the in-town, uptown Hurts. But the two names, Milne and Hurt, became inextricably linked in a scandalous love triangle that rocked the Casper community the night that Joel Hurt shot and killed young William Milne across from the Senate Saloon on Center Street because of William's love affair with Hurt's wife, Ettie.

The *Natrona Tribune* later covered the tragedy with remarkable restraint and sympathy for Joel Hurt, despite the fact that the paper had lambasted Hurt and his Democratic politics regularly for at least a year prior to the murder. The *Tribune* was a staunchly Republican publication, while the *Wyoming Derrick* was just as staunchly Democratic. The *Derrick,* in fact, beginning with its first issue on May 21, 1890, was owned by the Natrona County Publishing Company, whose five stockholders included Joel Hurt. When the editor and business manager, W.S. Kimball, retired to go into the drugstore business in June 1891, Hurt bought up all the stock, becoming sole owner. He then leased out the operation of the paper until prominent Casper attorney Alex T. Butler bought it in 1892. Meanwhile, the *Natrona Tribune* (which became the *Natrona County Tribune* in 1897 after purchase by A.J. Mokler) began operation in 1891, owned by twenty men who called themselves the Republican Publishing Company. Hence the battle lines were drawn, politically and editorially.

Both newspapers faithfully reported on the comings and goings of Casperites. Anyone who was interested could find out almost anything about the affairs of the townspeople—right down to how someone was feeling and what was being done about it.

The Hurt family figured prominently in these writings. Joel Hurt, prosperous sheepman that he was, had a magnificent home in Casper to accommodate his wife Ettie and six children—three boys and three girls ranging in age from three to nineteen—in addition to boarders (at least for a time) and a live-in servant. This very large and pretentious dwelling, built by Hurt, stood on the west side of what is now South Durbin Street between Second and First Streets. It is described by Frances Seely Webb in *Casper's First Homes* as having a full basement, living room, library or office, kitchen, pantry, and dining room on the first floor. Above the second-floor bedrooms was an attic—a rarity in the early houses of Casper, according to Webb. Large porches around the house added an elegant touch. The house boasted Casper's first bathtub with running water. Of course, it was just cold water; the hot water had to be heated on the coal range. The water was supplied by a windmill in the backyard, which also accounted for the fact that the Hurts had the first lawn in town, complete with trees.

However, Hurt didn't seem to spend much time at his palatial home. He was continually out of town on business. Mrs. Hurt did her share of traveling too, sometimes taking the children. A note in the *Wyoming Derrick* on December 31, 1891, stated that Mrs. Hurt and family had left for Denver where Freddie, nineteen, and Warren, seventeen, the two oldest sons, would attend school for the rest of the winter. And, in February 1892, the paper reported that Mrs. Hurt had just returned from ten days in Norfolk, Nebraska, where she had gone to take care of her husband who had been very ill with the "grippe," but had fully recovered.

Joel Hurt spent time in Norfolk because he had a large flock of sheep there, in addition to all those he ran in the Casper and Douglas areas. In fact, it was Joel Hurt who had trailed the first flock of sheep, three thousand strong, into Natrona County in 1888.

The paper noted his return to Casper from Norfolk on April 18, 1892, remarking that he was not yet looking well and that he expected to be at home for some time since the sheep were thriving and the shearing was proceeding nicely in Douglas, as well as in Norfolk.

The next week the paper again reported on Hurt's ill health, opining that he and the family would probably spend the summer on the Pacific coast.

In September of the next year the *Tribune* noted that Hurt, his children and a Miss Emma Daniels left to join Mrs. Hurt in Chicago; on October 26, it reported that Mrs. Hurt returned from Chicago bringing a niece and a nephew with her. November saw Hurt tending his sheep in both Casper and Norfolk, and Mrs. Hurt visiting in Chadron, Nebraska.

On November 16, the *Tribune* reported that Hurt and a man named Taylor had procured a "number of finest mutton sheep in the market and will in the future devote considerable attention to the breeding of sheep for mutton." It might have occurred to the interested reader that perhaps Joel Hurt lavished more time and attention on his sheep than he did upon his family, most notably his wife. A note in the paper innocently—or maybe not so innocently—pointed out in December that Mrs. Hurt had entertained the young people of Casper on Saturday evening at an enjoyable taffy pull at *her* home.

In late December the paper noted that son Fred Hurt was spending the holidays at home and that little Josie Hurt was in a children's Christmas program at the town hall, reciting a piece entitled "A Carol." Fred Hurt was one of the "eligible gentlemen" at Casper's Columbus Club Ball, billed as "the most brilliant society event in the history of central Wyoming." In addition to escorting his mother to the ball, he squired her to a birthday bash honoring another prominent Casperite, P. A. Demorest.

Joel Hurt apparently missed all this holiday festivity, not getting home from Norfolk until the end of January. But he did take Ettie to the next month's Columbus Ball where she wore "a charming toilette of black silk and lace."

The Columbus Club Balls were the brainchild of the ever-involved attorney Alex T. Butler. He organized a series of four or five of these midwinter galas which the *Tribune* raved about, touting Casper as the social arbiter of the entire state. For the February 1894 "masque Ball," attended by "the elite of Casper," Joel Hurt was in town and able to escort Ettie who went dressed as a "Spanish tambourine girl" in a daring ensemble.

Somehow, despite Hurt's frequent and lengthy absences from Casper, he found the time to indulge in local politics and run for mayor. Running for office in Casper was definitely not for the weak-hearted or the thin-skinned. Political races were hotly contested—no holds barred. Hurt first ran for mayor in May 1890 in the town's second election. He lost, getting sixty-six votes to the victor's seventy-two.

Local office holders were elected on a yearly basis. Hurt ran again, as a Democrat, of course, and the *Tribune* went after him. Unfortunately, copies of the *Derrick* from this time period were not preserved, so all accounts of local politics now must be interpreted from the writings in the *Tribune* which did its best to badmouth not only Hurt but the *Derrick* too. Hurt lost again.

Casper held its third municipal election on May 8, 1894. The *Tribune* reported that the turnout was the largest in town history. Two hundred thirty-three people voted, a large number of whom were sworn in at the polls since they had failed to register previously.

The results of the election were a big surprise: the Democratic candidate, Joel Hurt, upset the Republican apple cart. The *Tribune* reported that the campaign was the most heated ever held in Casper and scolded that the Republicans were caught napping and unprepared for the unexpected. Hurt received 138 votes for mayor, his opponent, C.K. Bucknum, ninety-five.

Mayor Hurt was installed into office on June 4, 1894, and from this point on the *Tribune* took a special interest in Joel J.

This picture was probably taken from the Old Grand Central Hotel corner facing east on Second Street on the occasion of the Gros Ventres and Sioux Indians passing through Casper on their way to Montana in about 1891. The man standing in the foreground near the center wearing a vest is believed to be J.J. Hurt. (Blackmore Collection: courtesy Casper College Library)

Hurt and his activities in a most uncomplimentary way. Its columns began to refer to him as the "Duke of Casper" and painted him, more or less, as a big-mouthed, obnoxious charlatan. In fact, a note in the June 28 edition—after quoting the *Cheyenne Sun* which surmised that Hurt had his eye on the governorship—accused Hurt of buying the mayor's post: "Peculiar financial management sometimes wins in municipal contests but such tactics cannot be brought into play in the State campaign—first because the pocket book is not long enough and second, because principles will be of more service—hence Joe has no cinch on even 'climbing in the window.'"

No doubt about it, really: Hurt was what one might refer to today as an "operator." He had his fingers in many pies. He was a director of the Casper Board of Trade. When Casper's School

District Number Two was formed in 1890 and a special election was held to bond the district in the amount of four thousand dollars to build a school, Hurt bought all the bonds. Although twenty Casper men signed a note guaranteeing to pay back the money if the district couldn't, the district had no trouble paying. When one of the school trustees resigned in August 1890, Hurt was elected to fill the vacancy. And when the Casper Lodge Number Fifteen of the Masons was organized in 1893, Hurt became a senior steward.

It was in 1894 that Mayor Hurt conceived the notion of establishing a wool scouring and knitting plant in Casper. With a plant like that he could maximize his own wool profits. So in June 1894, after selling stock in the venture, he traveled to North Galveston, Texas, to inspect such a facility whose machinery was for sale. He found the machinery to be obsolete and when he returned to Casper the *Tribune* reported, "It has not been definitely settled whether the Casper Wool Scouring and Knitting Company, as incorporated, will purchase new machinery and establish the business as originally intended, or whether the Company will disorganize and dissolve." Presenting Hurt's scouring plant as a pie-in-the-sky scheme, the paper went so far as to ridicule him by relating a personal conversation someone overheard on the train which carried Hurt to Galveston. Under a headline that pronounced "Will Have Him in Jail," it said:

> The following story is related of the "Duke of Casper" during his recent trip to a southern city on the ostensible mission of purchasing a scouring plant. To while away the time on the Elkhorn "flyer" his highness engaged in conversation with another passenger, and after proudly informing his new acquaintance that he was the great "Duke of Casper" and had just been elected mayor, he proceeded to unfold the secrets of the wonderful scheme that was to revolutionize the West and of which he was the star actor, and the man that supplied the wind. In the course of time

the subscription list was produced, and each subscriber for stock was discussed. Coming down to a certain name, his "duke ship" is said to have remarked, "Now there's a man that has subscribed for ____ shares of stock—I know he hasn't got a dollar—I'll have that feller in jail for doing that when I get back."

On the heels of this stirring gossip, the paper gave Hurt the dickens for letting the state Democratic convention slip through Casper's fingers to land in Cheyenne, despite the fact that Casper was hosting the state Republican convention in August. "Judging by his failures since his elevation to the office of Mayor of Casper, Joel J. Hurt must be a poor and unreliable score-keeper for his cuckoo organ authoritatively states that never in his life has that gentleman 'scored' a failure. The public will now keep score, and the first record will be the failure to establish the 'sure thing' scouring-knitting-woolen plant. The second, the failure to secure Casper the Democratic State Convention." (Hurt proved to be a gracious and efficient mayoral host to the Republican convention when it met in Casper and was actually complimented for his efforts by the *Tribune*.)

Besides being mayor of Casper, Joel Hurt was also a Wyoming state senator. He first won his senate seat in 1892 and was re-elected in 1894. Now, with the rumors of his aspiration to be governor, the paper had more fuel for its fire. It speculated on August 2 about whether Hurt would do the honorable thing and tender his resignation as state senator, or whether he would wait until after the Democratic state convention "so if he don't get the nomination he wants, he will still have something to cling to."

The *Tribune* wrote further: "Joel J. Hurt was placed before the democracy of Wyoming last week as an avowed candidate for congressman. Is there any other office for which he might be announced? Guess not unless there can be some other new office manufactured...to announce the great Natrona war horse for."

The August 30 edition of the paper mentioned that Hurt was off to Nebraska on business once again—and on September 6 a cryptic note asked, "How much does J.J. Hurt want to pay for the 100,000 sheep he has orders for, 50 cents per head?"

All this rhetoric described a man who was positively under siege publicly and, though the townspeople probably didn't know it yet, he was under siege privately, too. It may have been about this time that he discovered his wife's love affair with his sheep partner William "Billy" Milne, who boarded with the family from time to time. On the other hand, he may have been the last to know.

How Hurt found out about the affair between Ettie and Billy remains a matter for speculation, but the *Tribune's* accounts of Milne's murder the following April (1895) said the "proof" of the "intimacy...was so plain and absolute it drove him [Hurt] distracted. He left his home and children last September on a plea of ill health, to the detriment of his peace of mind and business interests, returning a week or two since"—which would have been in March 1895. While he was gone, according to those same reports, Hurt had his business agent settle "the business relations between the two men, leaving no excuse for Milne's further visits to the premises in the capacity of a property associate." This dissolution may have occurred in late October 1894, when the paper tersely noted that Hurt had returned to the city. Contrary to its usual policy where Hurt was concerned, it gave no details at all.

Hurt's tardy actions and efforts to erase William Milne from his beleaguered existence didn't succeed. Ettie and Billy continued their headlong and destructive affair, an episode of which a boarder at the Hurt home testified about at Hurt's trial.

This boarder, a Mrs. Webel, seems to have kept a very interested eye on the two lovers who, for their parts, couldn't have cared less about Mrs. Webel's interest.

Mrs. Webel recounted that on Thanksgiving eve, 1894, Ettie Hurt excused herself rather early in the evening to retire to

Joel J. and Ettie Hurt. (Hannah Rhoades McClure Album, Anderson Collection: courtesy Casper College Library)

the office in the house to write letters. Later on, after Mrs. Webel had gone to bed, she heard Ettie open the hall door and let Billy Milne into the house. She knew it was Billy and Ettie, she said, because she recognized their voices. Listening, she heard them go into Ettie's bedroom. She heard Billy's boots drop to the floor as if, she said, he was preparing for bed.

Mrs. Webel, who must have stayed awake most of the night, later heard one of the Hurts' little daughters (the three girls ranged in age from three to ten) awaken and ask her mother, "Momma, who is in bed with you?"

Ettie, Mrs. Webel said, immediately began to quiet the little girl, and much later—early the next morning—Billy left Ettie's room and went quietly to the bedroom that he was supposed to occupy when he stayed in the house.

The next night, Mrs. Webel went to church—no doubt to pray for guidance—and returned to the house where she found Ettie in bed and the lights turned low.

Mrs. Webel also retired to her bedroom, but not to bed. She must have made up her mind to put a stop to further adulterous carrying on, so she left her bedroom door ajar and settled in to wait.

It wasn't long before she heard Billy Milne come in the hall door. Once again she recognized his voice, and as he slipped by her bedroom, he reached out—Mrs. Webel said she saw his arm—and softly closed her bedroom door.

Ettie and Billy once again went into Ettie's bedroom, closing that door. Obviously, enough was enough as far as Mrs. Webel was concerned. She roused the servant woman, probably to act as a witness, and proceeded into the hall where she confronted Ettie, who must have heard the commotion and gotten herself and Billy out of bed.

Mrs. Webel accused Ettie to her face of sleeping with Billy. Ettie denied it.

Mrs. Webel then ran to Milne's room and burst in—to find Billy taking off his clothes. Unfortunately, Mrs. Webel's trial testimony stopped at that point, maybe because she had quickly moved out of that house of sin, or maybe Ettie had put her out. And it was probably Mrs. Webel who let a lot of Casper in on the "intimacy" that was "so plain and absolute."

Ettie Hurt did a bit of talking on her own that she shouldn't have done. She should have known better; she was probably about forty years old at the time since she had a son who was nineteen. Mrs. Hurt told a former servant woman that "no living woman is good enough for Billy Milne, and if I ever have another child I hope he will be the father of it." And to a male acquaintance she expressed the hope that someone would shoot her husband Joel. Both of these people repeated her statements at Joel's trial.

Hurt returned to Casper in late March 1895, from wherever he had been, but he didn't return to his house. The *Tribune* reported that in the week or two he'd been back, Hurt had sent numerous messages to Billy Milne to "keep away from his house and keep his [Milne's] stock out of his [Hurt's] stables."

Milne, in effect, told Hurt to go fly a kite, more specifically, to "come and put us out." And Milne, the paper said, threatened Hurt with bodily harm if the two should happen to meet. It was because of these threats that William Hodge advised Hurt to arm himself—as Hodge testified at the trial. The paper further reported that Hurt met frequently with his children and declared that he was "devotedly attached" to them and held "only pity" for Ettie's "ignorance and sorrow for her indiscretion."

The Hurt marriage spanned twenty years or more and it seems clear that Ettie had grown bored and resentful of an absentee husband whose priorities and projects ignored or discounted her in almost every way and, regardless of what the paper said, probably the children, too. Young and vibrant, Billy Milne was, tragically, in the wrong place at the wrong time and much too eager to participate in his own destruction, probably never believing that he wasn't invulnerable and the master of his fate.

On the evening of April 3, 1895, Billy Milne, in what was his established routine, rode into Casper, put his horse in the Hurt stable and ate supper at the house. Some time afterward he went uptown ending up at the Grand Central Hotel on the southwest corner of Second and Center Streets. Joel Hurt was also at the Grand Central—perhaps he was lodging there—and it seems inevitable that the two men would run into each other.

About nine o'clock, according to the *Tribune,* a witness named Bryant, who was on the street near the hotel, saw Milne come out of the building and turn in the direction of the nearby Senate Saloon. Hurt followed Milne out, approached him by the alley between the Cunningham store and Seely's gun shop, tapped him on the shoulder, and said, "Turn face around."

Milne turned, saw Hurt, and immediately went for his gun. But he was too slow. From a distance of less than nine feet, Hurt fired two or three shots—witness accounts varied. Some said Milne fired a shot, too; others said he did not.

Milne partly ran, partly staggered across the street into the Senate Saloon, where he collapsed and uttered his last words: "My God, I was too slow." (Here, too, reports differ. Mokler's history records Milne's last words as, "My God, I'm shot." In *Casper's First Homes,* Webb declares that Hurt then said he would "cut his heart out," even though eyewitnesses denied he said it.)

Another witness to the shooting approached Milne, turned him over and saw that he was dead. One bullet had passed directly through his heart.

Billy Milne was twenty-seven years old.

Hurt was arrested and put in jail. His arraignment was held within a few days before Justice of the Peace William Ford and the huge crowd who turned out for it.

Hurt pled not guilty to murder. His lawyers tried to argue that Hurt fired in self-defense and that, therefore, the shooting was justifiable homicide. That didn't work, and neither did the motion to discharge him: both pleas were denied by Justice Ford.

After the prosecuting attorneys—George Walker and Alex T. Butler of Columbus Club Ball fame—finished their well-prepared arguments, Hurt was bound over for trial in the district court which would convene in May. The charge was manslaughter. His bail was set at five thousand dollars, which was readily paid, and he was released. The decision of the court was greeted with cheers and applause, and Justice Ford had to threaten one onlooker with contempt of court before he could restore order.

The *Tribune* did a complete about-face concerning its policy of lambasting Joel Hurt in its pages and now declared a hands-off policy. It intended to refer only briefly "to the particulars of the sad affair which has so recently occurred in our midst," explaining that the "president of this company [the *Tribune*] is so intimately connected with the case in its legal aspect as to render it manifestly improper for this paper to draw upon the facts as drawn out at the coroner's inquest or the preliminary examination. And besides, it seems improper to any extent to forestall the action of the courts in any case, much less a case as important as this one is." (The paper's owner was named O.A. Hamilton, but the link between him and Hurt is uncertain.) However, the item went on, it was not improper to report that "the decision of Judge Ford meets with substantially the unanimous approval of the people of this community," and that "practically the entire community sympathizes deeply with senator Hurt without regard to politics or the relations which have heretofore existed between him and the individuals which go to make up the community."

The paper also carried the following notice: "The family of William Milne desire through the *Tribune* to extend their thanks to the friends who kindly assisted in the burial of their son and brother. Especial thanks are extended to the Odd Fellows of the city of Casper." It was signed by either Billy's brother or his father (both named James).

Billy Milne was buried in Casper's Highland Cemetery, which had only been established the year before. His marker in the family plot, now tilting and peeling from age and weather, was large and eloquent for its day. It reads, "Sacred to the Memory of William/Second Son of James and Jane H. Milne/ Age 27 Years/Late of Aberdeen, Scotland."

Hurt's trial was held in the district court in Casper in late May 1895. Judge Hayford presided over the proceedings which took only a brief two or three days, after which the jury needed only five minutes to declare Joel Hurt innocent by reason of "emotional insanity which rendered him irresponsible for his acts." (Mokler remarked in his history that "Mr. Hurt's mind was soon 'restored.'")

As a free man Hurt went right on with his usual business activities. He had not run for mayor again since that race took

The lobby of the Grand Central Hotel. Hugh "Colorado" Patton, the owner, stands at left. Mrs. Patton is in doorway at rear. (Frances Seely Webb Collection: courtesy Casper College Library)

place while he was embroiled in his trial, and a new mayor was installed in June 1895.

Hurt wasted no time, though, in filing a divorce action against Ettie, notice of which appeared in the *Tribune* on May 30, 1895. Though many predicted the divorce proceedings would occur in Casper, they did not. The case was heard in Cheyenne. Hurt's attorneys went there as well as to Laramie, where apparently some of the papers had been filed.

The preliminary action in the divorce case took place in August. At that time, Ettie Hurt petitioned the court to allow her twenty-five hundred dollars in attorney fees—in addition to a monthly allowance until the divorce was settled. The court ruled to grant her a $150 monthly allowance and $750 for attorney fees, not a paltry sum by that day's standards. Neither Ettie nor Joel was present at this proceeding.

The Hurts' divorce was a bitterly fought action. Petitions flew back and forth like well-aimed snowballs, most of them lobbed by Joel, who had made up his mind to win the battle.

The first petition was filed in the First Judicial District of Laramie County in Cheyenne. In it Joel was given custody of the three boys and Ettie was given custody of the three girls. The judge warned, however, that Casper would not be an appropriate place to raise the girls because they would be continually subject to finger pointing, gossip, and ridicule.

Ettie was awarded an alimony amounting to twenty-five dollars a month in addition to fifty dollars a month for the maintenance and education of the girls. These amounts were a far cry from the first magnanimous bequests, but Ettie also got to keep the Casper house. In addition, the judge ruled that Joel must pay Ettie's attorney's fees—undoubtedly a practical decision to assure that her lawyers got paid, since Ettie, certainly, couldn't have had much money of her own.

The divorce was final on September 29, 1896. Sometime subsequent to that, Joel filed a supplemental action in which he accused Ettie, who was still living in Casper, of associating with disreputable persons, "thereby surrounding said children with evil and corrupt influence and blighting their future prospects in life."

His petition further stated that during this time Ettie had met a disreputable person in Casper named Lon Schaeffer who was a convicted felon, not long out of the penitentiary where he had been serving a sentence for grand larceny. (Apparently Ettie was using the big house in Casper as a boarding house and had allegedly rented Mr. Schaeffer a room.) The petition stated that "the children are humiliated and disgraced and are subjected to the vile, degrading and pernicious influence of Lon Schaeffer." Now a hearing was set to determine whether the original decree

This is the home that Joel Hurt built. After the Hurts lived here it had a number of owners or tenants, including J. V. Cantlin, Dr. John F. Leeper, and Charles Bucknum. At some point in time, possibly in the twenties or thirties, the house was moved up Second Street to 1023 East Second. There it became an apartment house which was called the Lovelace Apartments for many, many years. It was demolished in the late 1980s having become extremely decrepit. A used car lot is in its place now. (Frances Seely Webb Collection: courtesy Casper College Library)

should be modified. Joel wanted the girls given to him and the alimony stopped.

Ettie's reply denied all of Joel's allegations. She declared that Lon Schaeffer was merely a boarder in her house and paid rent for the room he occupied. She stated that although Mr. Schaeffer had been convicted of grand larceny, he had been pardoned by the Governor of Wyoming and, furthermore, *he* had never been charged with murder for shooting someone in the back. Joel had. She scored a direct hit with that statement.

The judge, nevertheless, modified his decree and gave custody of the girls to Joel and discontinued all the monetary payments to Ettie.

Joel counted an additional victory when he won back the palatial family home. Ettie had sold the house to a man by the name of Robert Taylor for a paltry sum of money. (This Taylor may have been the same Taylor who had invested in sheep with Hurt.) Taylor said he had bought the house just as a favor to Ettie, but Joel declared that Taylor stole the property. Hurt raised such a ruckus that Taylor let him have it back—and good riddance.

Joel Hurt remained in Casper for some years, conducting his business in his usual volatile manner. At one point he successfully sued the county commissioners for several hundred dollars he said they owed him. Later, in turn, a Casper business sued Hurt for several hundred dollars which they said he owed *them* for supplies—and they got their money.

Mokler's *History of Natrona County* notes that after several years Hurt moved to Omaha.

Ettie Hurt moved to Cheyenne and married, becoming Mrs. Lon Schaeffer.

CHAPTER FIVE

⌐ ⌐ ⌐ ⌐ ⌐ ⌐ ⌐ ⌐ ⌐ ⌐ ⌐

THREE TRIALS
AND HE'S FREE

KENNETH MCRAE WAS a prosperous sheepman who ran a sheep camp at Fales Creek at the foot of the Rattlesnake Mountains sixty miles west of Casper. Fales Creek can be found today by driving out the Poison Spider Road almost to the Six-Mile Ranch.

McRae's misadventure into infamy happened on a Sunday morning, May 30, 1897, when he allegedly shot and killed one of his several sheepherders, a young Scotsman named Robert Gordon. Twenty-seven years old, Gordon hailed from Roschire, Scotland, and had been in Wyoming only about a year. He was, evidently, not one of McRae's favorite employees. It's not clear why, but for as much as a week prior to the murder, McRae had been cursing Gordon and threatening to beat him to death with a club.

Peter Keith, another sheepherder working for McRae, had warned Gordon of McRae's threats but didn't really think he was deadly serious. Because of the threats, Gordon made himself scarce around the sheep camp. Or perhaps his absence was due to the instructions given him by McRae to go to the Souter sheep camp, which was not far away, to get some whiskey.

At about five o'clock on the Sunday morning of the murder, herder Peter Keith—who was also camp cook—returned to camp from wherever he had been and looked around, but didn't see Gordon. He asked McRae, who was lying in his sheep wagon, where Gordon was.

McRae said, according to Keith's later censored court testimony, "That — — — has not brought me my whiskey. I will never be satisfied until I have that — — — — heart's blood."

Keith then fixed McRae's breakfast. He put some extra food on the stove and said to McRae, "This is Gordon's breakfast."

McRae said, "That — — — —will never eat here, anymore."

Keith kept his bedroll under the supply wagon and went there to lie down. Hearing some movement, he looked out and saw that Gordon had returned. He watched as Gordon went into McRae's sheep wagon. McRae began to curse at him and wanted to know where the whiskey was. Gordon replied that he had been watching the sheep.

McRae said, "You — — —, what is it to you where the sheep went to?"

Gordon then said he'd go for the whiskey right away, but Keith couldn't hear McRae's reply. Since he didn't hear any more talking, Keith dropped off to sleep.

The next thing he knew, there was a loud noise and a man screamed, "Peter! Peter! I am shot! I am shot!"

The shouts were Gordon's and Keith ran to him. Gordon had staggered several feet from McRae's wagon where he fell on his knees. Apparently Keith grabbed him because Gordon fell over Keith. Keith turned him over and looked at his face, yelling to McRae that Gordon was hurt.

McRae came out of his sheep wagon after a minute and stood about six feet away from the two men.

Keith said to him, "Surely to God you haven't shot this boy, have you?" McRae was carrying a .45-70 Winchester rifle, holding it with both hands.

"I was trying to push him out of the wagon with the rifle, and the gun went off and shot him," McRae said.

Keith told McRae to go get some water. McRae returned with the water in one hand, the rifle in the other and stood again six feet back.

Keith said, "He is dead."

"What will we do with him?" McRae asked.

Keith replied, "He is dead and we can't do nothing with him."

McRae then wanted Keith to find someone named John Landon—probably a fellow sheepman who had a camp in the vicinity. Keith refused because he didn't know where Landon was, but said he would go get Souter, whose camp was close by and known to him.

William Clark, another of McRae's herders who had witnessed parts of the activities, said to McRae, "My God, Mac, what have you done?"

According to the newspaper report, McRae replied, "Ain't it fearful—ain't it fearful? It will cause me lots of trouble, but I've got a clear conscience."

McRae then told Clark a different story, saying that the gun was lying on the bed where either he or Gordon (reports are unclear) had thrown it—next to a shotgun which was already lying on the bed—and that the Winchester discharged, shooting Gordon. The Winchester was McRae's gun.

By this time several men had arrived, and they helped get the flies off the terrible wound in Gordon's chest. They wrapped the body in a tarpaulin and laid it under the supply wagon.

McRae now told Pat Fagan, another sheepman on the scene, that when Gordon pitched the gun onto the bed next to the shotgun it went off and shot him. McRae said, further, that he would put the body in a wagon and bring it to Casper, but first he asked Fagan what he thought about the whole thing.

Fagan told McRae that, under the circumstances, he thought there should be a coroner's investigation.

McRae, for whatever reasons, didn't get Gordon's body to Casper until three days later, June 2.

The coroner's jury brought in the following verdict on June 7: "We, the coroner's jury impaneled to investigate into the cause of death of Robert Gordon on Sunday, the 30th day of May, 1897, find from the testimony of the witnesses that Robert Gordon came to his death from a gun shot wound from a gun in the hands of Kenneth McRae."

At the preliminary hearing two days later, the witnesses gave essentially the same testimony all over again and were strenuously cross-examined.

Afterwards, a *Natrona County Tribune* reporter attending the hearing asked McRae for a statement and was told in no uncertain terms by his lawyer that McRae would make no remarks for publication.

McRae pled not guilty to the murder.

Sometime during this interval Pat Fagan asked Peter Keith if he would return to McRae's sheep camp. Keith said he would not because he was afraid to, so Fagan told him he could come to his own camp to work.

According to the *Natrona County Tribune* report, McRae resided in the county jail until his trial on the first-degree murder charges began in district court on January 17, 1898. The newspaper described his appearance:

> When McRae was brought into the court room his appearance was greatly changed from that of a few months ago, being very pale and thin, and somewhat nervous, due, presumably, from his close confinement in the county jail. When the jury was called up and sworn he eyed the twelve very closely, and listened very attentively to every question and answer that was asked by the attorneys and jurors. He showed no signs, however of being displeased or in favor of any of the jurors and talesmen examined, but sat in his chair with his hands clasped together and rocked to and fro, seemingly unconcerned as to who was excused or who was retained.

The selection of his jury became a marathon of challenges by both the state and the defense. Many prospective jurors seemed to have already formed firm opinions as to McRae's guilt or innocence from reading the extensive coverage in the Casper papers—which sold like hotcakes whenever they carried reports about evidence in the case. In fact, Judge Brown rather severely chastised the papers for printing "purported evidence." The *Tribune* shot back that all the gossip surrounding the case did much more to sway opinion than the paper, which reported *only* the facts. At any rate, jury selection took very nearly three full court days: seventy-one men were examined before the final twelve were chosen.

The case opened on Thursday morning, January 20. On the following Monday, after thirty-six hours of deliberation, after twenty ballots ranging from a unanimous decision against first-degree murder to the final ballot of eight for acquittal and four for conviction, the jury threw in the towel and declared it could not come to an agreement. Judge Brown dismissed the jury and ordered a new trial which was to begin a week later.

Kenneth McRae was released on a bond of thirty thousand dollars and was ordered to appear in court every morning until his new trial began.

This time, Judge Charles W. Bramel, of the second judicial district, decided to see to it that the newspapers didn't muddy up the waters—that is, rehash all the evidence. He asked them to refrain from printing everything they knew, so that an impartial jury wouldn't be impossible to impanel for the second trial.

This second trial seems to have actually begun on Friday, February 4, according to the *Tribune*. Seventy-five men were called for jury duty and due, perhaps, to Judge Bramel's far-sightedness, only forty-four men were examined before the jury was seated.

It was from this trial that the *Tribune* printed McRae's own account of Gordon's death.

My name is Kenneth McRae; I am 32 or 33 years old,
I don't know which, live in Natrona County, Wyoming;
have lived here seven years, but came to the state in 1889;
lived in Carbon County before I came here. Have been in
the sheep business during residence in Natrona County.
Knew Robert Gordon since first week in July, 1896;
worked for me from 11th day of July, 1896, till the day he
died; had a friendly feeling toward him; he was running
my outfit in my absence and during my sickness. I was in
bed at the time he died, and was sick eight or nine days
before, and was confined to my bed five days before. I was
going to be absent some time from the 6th day of June
and had made arrangements with Gordon to take care of
my sheep and my business during my absence. The day
before the shooting of Gordon occurred I sent him down
to Souter's camp. Souter told me he had some whiskey,
and I asked him to send me up some if he had any left. I
wanted the whiskey because I was sick. I had lost my dog
and had information that a man had the dog I had lost;
the man was going to leave that night or in the morning
and take my dog with him. The dog came home that
evening about an hour after Gordon had left camp. I saw
William Clark that night after dark; he asked me how I
was feeling and I said better. He said, "I see Bess [the dog]
is back again," and asked if Bob [Gordon] knew that Bess
was home. I said no, and then made some swearing; I
used ugly words and was angry with the man for getting
away with my dog; did not mention Gordon's name when
I was swearing; I was swearing at the man (I didn't know
his name) who had the dog. The principle thing that
made me mad, I thought Gordon would go after the dog
in the morning and keep him away from work. I laid back
in bed and said "G—d—n," and repeated "G—d—n that
s— of a b——. If I had gone down there I would kill the

s— of a b——." I did not intend to kill anybody but said that to give expression to my anger at the man who had Bess; was not angry at Robert Gordon.... The first man to camp in the morning was Peter Keith. He ate breakfast and gave me some coffee. He asked if Gordon would be in for breakfast. I said, "I don't think Gordon will be in here for breakfast because he will go after the dog from Souter's camp." I made no threats that morning. After Keith went to bed Gordon came in to camp about 8 o'clock. He told me that Bess had come back. After that we talked of matters what was to be done with the sheep during the day. We talked about a quarter of an hour, when the stove began to get warm, and I turned over on my right side in the bed, toward the near end of the wagon to go to sleep. Do not know how long I was there before I heard the report of the gun and heard Gordon shout, "I'm shot! I'm shot!" It was Gordon on the floor of the wagon the first I saw of him. He first appeared to make a jump toward the door of the wagon, and then disappeared out the door. I got out of bed as quick as I could and saw him partly under the supply wagon near Peter Keith's bed, with his head down and his arms under his breast. I went out and turned him over and called to Peter that Gordon had been shot. I called him the second time. Had no gun in my hand. When I went back into the wagon I looked at the foot of the bed and saw the rifle and shot gun lying there with the muzzle pointing toward the door. That is where the guns are usually kept. The guns were used to scare coyotes. I used the gun that morning to turn a bunch sheep that was on the other side of the creek. When I fired the gun the sheep, which were going away, checked up a little and commenced to graze... Put the gun back on the foot of the bed again after I used it...Think I loaded it that morning. Went out and turned Gordon over. Don't know what Keith said when he first woke up, but when he looked at Gordon he said: "He has just fainted, man; bring some water;" when I came back with the water I saw that Gordon was dead. The gun was in the wagon, and I did not have the gun in my hand when I brought the water. I suppose the gun was in the wagon...

I had nothing to do with the killing of Robert Gordon. I believe that it happened by him moving the gun in some way, because I felt the jar on my feet. I showed Pat Fagan, Sam Hanes, Wm. Clark and Charles Souter how I thought it happened. When I showed them I think I said: It must have happened this way, but did not claim to any one to know how it happened. I had conversation with Wm. Clark that morning, and the first thing he said to me was: "My God, Mac, it is an awful job." I said, "It is fearful," and repeated it. Then we talked about what was to be done with the sheep. Then I asked if he thought it best to take the body to town, and how many days it would take to send a man to town and then come back and take the body to town. Then we saw some freighters on the road and I said, "Let's go down and see what they think about it." When I got town [*sic*] there I told one of the men that a man at my camp got shot that morning and wanted to know what was usually done in such cases, and asked him if he would take the body to town, and he said that if I was sure it was not suicide he would take the body to town. I did not tell Clark not to say anything about what I had said the night before. I said nothing to Keith about shoving Gordon out of the wagon with the gun, and it is not true that I shoved him out of the wagon with the gun. After the men [Fagan, Hanes, etc.] came to the camp we looked at the wound and found it was fly-blowed and then cut out a piece of the shirt and put some coal oil on the wound, then we wrapped him up in a canvas, put him below the supply wagon and put some quilts and tarpaulin around the wagon so the sun could not shine in.

On Friday morning, a week later, the jury reached its verdict. The news spread like wildfire and the courtroom was jammed by the time the court officials, the jury, and the defendant arrived. (McRae had been eating breakfast with friends in the Grand Central Hotel dining room.)

The clerk of the court read the verdict to a hushed courtroom: "State of Wyoming versus Kenneth McRae. We the jury, in the above titled case, find the defendant, Kenneth McRae, guilty of murder in the first degree, as charged in the indictment."

McRae, the *Tribune* reported, "was stunned and sank to his chair as though his knees had given way." The courtroom audience seemed similarly stunned. McRae's lawyers immediately informed the court that they would file a motion for a new trial, and then McRae was ordered to the county jail. The paper noted that on the march to the jail, McRae spoke not a word.

The next day the judge set the hearing on the motion for a new trial for March 11, but later it was postponed until April.

The *Tribune* had reported in its February 17 edition that McRae's attitude was one of nonchalance, although he apparently remained adamant—as he had been all through his second trial—about taking further action if he was, indeed, found guilty. The *Tribune* further reported that "the prisoner now spends most of his time [in jail] whistling and singing. He has a good appetite and sleeps well, but does a great deal of talking while asleep, but ever since he has been in jail he has done more or less talking in his sleep, and from all appearances he does not seem to be worried as to what the final outcome will be." The paper also rendered the opinion that "McRae, who less than a year ago was a wealthy 'flockmaster' is today financially ruined and broken down in spirit, and if innocent, nothing too great can be done to atone for the injury done him, but if guilty his punishment should fit the crime."

McRae's third trial took place in Rawlins, a change of venue. According to A.J. Mokler's *History of Natrona County* the Carbon County sheriff refused, at first, to lodge McRae in the Rawlins jail because he thought Natrona County was flat broke and couldn't pay for McRae's keep. That did not prove to be true although the cost of McRae's three trials did eventually cost the county more than six thousand dollars—which caused much bitter feeling among the Casper townspeople for a long time.

This third trial began on May 2, 1898. On June 2—one month later and one year after Robert Gordon's death—McRae was acquitted of the charge of first degree murder and set free "without prejudice."

Within one month of McRae's acquittal, a note of interest appeared in the *Tribune* on June 30, 1898: "The marriage of Miss Wilhelmina M. Clark to Kenneth McRae took place yesterday morning at 9:00 in the parlors of the Grand Central Hotel, Reverend E.P. Wells of Cheyenne officiating. The bride was attended by Miss Belle Clark as maid of honor and the groom by Mr. George Taylor as best man."

The bride was Superintendent of Schools for Natrona County at the time of her wedding.

Kenneth McRae did not live to be an old man. He died in 1913 at forty-eight or forty-nine years old; he and Wilhelmina were married only a short fifteen years. He is buried at Highland Cemetery between his wife, who died at a venerable eighty-six years of age in 1958, and Isabella M. McRae, born July 10, 1901, and deceased May 27, 1905—not quite four years old. Perhaps the child was their daughter, although Kenneth's obituary in the *Casper Press* of Friday, June 13, 1913, made no mention of a deceased child, saying: "Kenneth McRae, a sheepman, was brought to Casper last Friday suffering with an advantaged [*sic*] stage of mountain fever and was placed in the State hospital for treatment. He constantly grew worse and died at 2:00 on Monday afternoon.

"The funeral was conducted by Rev. L.W. Kingsley at the Methodist church on Wednesday morning at 10:00. Deceased leaves a widow and three daughters."

CHAPTER SIX

THE TRAIN ROBBERY

WHAT DRAMA CAPTURES the American imagination like a daring train robbery? Although this one took place outside of Casper, all the aftermath centered in and around the city, so Casper—like the hub of a wheel with spokes fanning out in every direction—was the focal point.

"Our town was thrown into great excitement," the *Natrona County Tribune* reported, by a crime committed at about two o'clock in the morning of Friday, June 2, 1899. The first section of the westbound Union Pacific Overland Flyer mail train was flagged down by a red lantern at Wilcox, a little station six or eight miles east of the old Rock Creek Station and about fourteen miles short of Medicine Bow. Two men jumped into the engine cab and ordered engineer W.R. Jones and his fireman to pull the train across the little wooden bridge just ahead. That done, the bridge was promptly dynamited, stranding the second section of the train, which was due within minutes. When the interlopers ordered the engineer to pull the train another mile up the track to conceal it from view, Jones refused and reportedly set the air brake. One of the robbers then attacked him viciously, pistol whipping him with his gun and threatening his life. The older of the two robbers restrained his companion by saying, "Don't kill him."

After the train was pulled out of sight, the pair and their cohorts turned their attention to the mail and express cars. It was the express car that held what they had come for: the money. The express messenger, a man named Woodcock, was ordered to open the door. When he refused, the robbers lost no time in dynamiting the car—which pretty effectively blew it to bits along with the safe inside. It turned out to be Mr. Woodcock's lucky night because he was only knocked out, not killed, by the explosion. The robbers were amply supplied with dynamite: at least one hundred pounds of it were later found near the scene.

The *Wyoming Derrick* in its June 8 edition carried a firsthand account of the robbery told by mail clerk, Robert Lawson, that differs in some details from the *Tribune's* version.

Lawson, too, recounted that the robbers went almost immediately up into the engine cab. Then he claimed they beat engineer "Grindstone" Jones, as he was known, and his fireman for moving too slowly as they were marched back to Lawson's mail car. There Lawson's boss, chief clerk Burt Bruce, refused to open the mail car's door. After about fifteen minutes shots were fired into the car, followed by a terrible explosion that forced everyone out of the mail car. The robbers said they didn't want the mail, they wanted what was in the express car, and they would blow up the whole train to get it if they needed to.

Right about then the outlaws saw the lights of the second section of the train approaching and asked what was on it. Some fast thinker said it carried two cars of soldiers. Scared, the robbers hurried their captives back to the engine, then drove it across a bridge over a gully and stopped. While some of the robbers uncoupled two of the train's extra cars, the others ran back to dynamite the bridge. Then they ran the train a couple of miles up the track. Now they concentrated on the express car. After blowing it up, they went for the other mail car and found no resistance there. Lawson said they blew up the safes last of all, tearing the express car to pieces. He said they took or destroyed everything from the safes. Postal clerk Lawson concluded:

After finishing their work they [the robbers] started in a northerly direction on foot.

In the meantime the second section [of the train] had crossed the bridge in safety, which, while not destroyed, was badly damaged. The passenger train then proceeded to the Wilcox sidetrack, where they waited for some time... At length they [train and personnel] proceeded and coming up to the scene of the holdup, viewed the surroundings and found behind a snow fence, blankets and quilts, as well as two sacks of giant powder, each about 50 pounds in weight.

The engine of the first section had been sent ahead to Aurora, the nearest telegraph station, from which place the alarm was sent out. We soon followed, dragging along the damaged express car which knocked against sign boards and switches.

The men all wore long masks reaching below their necks, and of three that I observed one looked to be six feet tall, the others being about ordinary sized men. The leader appeared to be about 50 years old, and spoke with a squeaky voice, pitched very high. They appeared not to want to unnecessarily hurt any one and were quite sociable and asked one of the boys for a chew of tobacco.

How much money did the robbers get away with? Many people speculated, and estimates ranged from a few thousand to as much as sixty thousand dollars with a high guess at a hundred thousand. A jagged piece of a one-hundred-dollar bill, found at the robbery site, only fueled the speculation.

The reward notice offered on June 10 by the Union Pacific Railroad, the Pacific Express Company, and the United States Government, listed thirty-four hundred dollars in unsigned currency notes from the First National Bank of Portland, Oregon. Actual cash money was not mentioned. Another, perhaps questionable, source is the unpublished manuscript *The Bandit Invincible: The Story of Butch Cassidy*, attributed to Cassidy himself, which sets the cash amount at forty-eight thousand dollars.

❖   ❖   ❖

For indeed, Cassidy was one of the band of six train robbers, although this wasn't yet known. And who were the rest?

Following the robbery the group must have retrieved their horses, and split up, because all subsequent newspaper accounts deal only with the three who headed for Casper. Their identities were not known at first, but it didn't take long for names to surface, even though the newspapers refrained from specifying them. The *Derrick* went so far as to say that the robbers' names were known, but doubt still reigned generally. Because of that, the paper cautioned, it was best to keep quiet for the moment.

There are a number of diverse and conflicting versions of the suspects' identities. Aliases and variant spellings add to the complexity. James D. Horan and Paul Sann, in their *Pictorial History of the Wild West,* identify four of them as members of Butch Cassidy's "Wild Bunch": Cassidy himself; George "Big Nose" Curry (whom the authors may have confused with the actual member of Cassidy's gang, George "Flat Nose" Currie); Harvey "Kid Curry" Logan; and Elza (Elzy) Lay. However, the reward notice, reprinted in their volume, states that evidence pointed to the brothers Louis "Lonie" Curry and Harvey "Kid" Curry (their actual last name, Logan, is not mentioned), and to R.E. Curry—not related—as three of the bandits.

Richard Patterson's book *Wyoming's Outlaw Days* identifies one of the robbers as Bob Lee (a cousin of Harvey and Lonie Logan) and offers the observation that "Some say that Butch may have helped plan it [the robbery] but did not participate in it."

The *Wyoming History News* of September 1994 carries an account by E.J. Farlow, an early Wyoming pioneer in and around Lander and an acquaintance of Cassidy. Farlow wrote that Butch was, indeed, one of the outlaws, and that Butch showed up in Lander after the robbery, where he hid out for two days in the back of a friend's saloon before going on to the Indian reservation to rest up for a couple of weeks at the ranch of a long-time

Harvey "Kid Curry" Logan was identified as being one of the six bandits who robbed the Overland Flyer near Wilcox. (Union Pacific Museum Collection)

friend, Emery Burnaugh. According to Burnaugh, Butch had forty thousand dollars on his person.

In his *History of Natrona County* Mokler wrote that three of the robbers were Harve (a.k.a. Kid Curry) Logan, one of the Roberts boys, and George Currie.

In *Powder River Country: The Papers of J. Elmer Brock*, Brock wrote that he personally knew the three outlaws being hunted by the posses: they were George Curry, Kid Curry (not related) and an experienced train robber, Harry Lonabaugh [Longabaugh] who was, of course, the Sundance Kid.

In the manuscript *The Bandit Invincible*, purportedly written by Cassidy himself and chronicled in Larry Pointer's book *In Search of Butch Cassidy*, the author wrote that Cassidy's partners in this crime were Dick Maxwell (the name he uses throughout his narrative for the Sundance Kid), Ben Kilpatrick (though he spells it Killpatrick), Dusty Bill Conner Odell, and Kid Curry, whom he mentioned as the robber who beat engineer Jones. Harvey Ray may have been the sixth member of the gang, but his identity is arguable.

❖　❖　❖

The sheriff's office in Casper got a telegram about the robbery late that same Friday, thanks to engineer Jones who, despite the assault on his person, ran fourteen miles to Medicine Bow to report the crime, according to the *Natrona County Tribune*. Because Oscar Hiestand, the Casper sheriff, was out of town on another manhunt, it fell to Deputy Sheriff Warren E. Tubbs to quickly gather a posse of seven and set out for Alcova, guarding the bridges along the way. The weather was awful, the rain was coming down in torrents, and they got lost. Finally, they managed to straggle back to town thirty-six hours later, a bedraggled and discouraged group whose search had been fruitless.

Saturday afternoon a train arrived in Casper with several officials, two of whom were Converse County Sheriff Joe Hazen and a Union Pacific detective named Vizzard, from Omaha.

After they had consulted for a few hours with Sheriff Hiestand, the train with its remaining passengers left for Cheyenne.

Telegrams flew between stations of the UP and Casper. Everyone in Casper and the entire state of Wyoming watched for a glimpse of the train robbers, who seemed to have disappeared into thin air.

However, a few night owls in Casper probably saw more than they realized at the time. Mokler wrote in his *History of Natrona County* that three of the train robbers—George Currie, Harve Logan, and one of the Roberts boys—rode into Casper Saturday night (June 3) for food and supplies, perhaps aided and abetted by George Currie's brother who was an employee of the Chicago and Northwestern Railroad roundhouse in Casper. The *Derrick* estimated that since the distance from the train robbery site to Casper was 110 miles, it would have taken the outlaws until two A.M. Sunday to reach town. They figured that from Bates Hole the robbers took a shortcut across the mountains, through the Hat Six Canyon, and across the foothills—proving their familiarity with this part of Wyoming.

The three men then came riding through town about two A.M. on Sunday, as leisurely as could be, past all the open saloons to Bucknum's livery stable. Unfortunately, the hostler there refused to get up to take care of their horses. As they passed by one of the still-open saloons someone was heard to say, "There's a chance to make a reputation. There go the train robbers," the Derrick reported later.

The bandits then rode on up the river and crossed the bridge without anyone looking twice. The paper went on to say that "the failure to guard the Casper Bridge across the Platte River on Saturday night, after notice had been received here to be on the lookout and men sent out to guard the crossings and avenues of escape, is more generally criticized than any other feature of the affair. It was certainly a blunder on the part of somebody, hard to understand."

The *Natrona County Tribune* said it later that week in head-lines: "Neglect of Detective Vizzard to Guard the Platte River Bridge Makes it Easy for the Men to Escape Into the Interior. Passed Through Casper Sunday Morning."

It wasn't until later that Sunday morning, June 4, that a re-port of a sighting of the robbers surfaced. A sheepherder named Al Hudspeth was out hunting for his horses about six miles northwest of the city along Casper Creek, near an old oil well and an abandoned cabin. As he approached the cabin he was surprised to see a man standing in the doorway watching him.

Hudspeth asked the fellow if he was the owner of the horses grazing on the nearby hill, because he (Hudspeth) had lost some. The fellow said, "Why in hell don't you go and see?"

Hudspeth was still trying to explain his problem when an-other man came out of the cabin carrying two Winchester rifles. He gave one to his companion who leveled it at Hudspeth and said, "Hit the road and do it damned quick!"

Hudspeth quit trying to be a nice guy and did exactly as he was told, racing straight back to Casper to the sheriff's office.

As soon as they heard Hudspeth's story, sheriffs Hiestand and Hazen organized a posse and lit out. It seemed the whole town wanted to go with them, but there was a severe shortage of horses. Sheriff Hiestand rode out to the CY ranch west of town to get extra mounts while Sheriff Hazen galloped off with six good men. Hiestand soon followed with three more men, mak-ing a total of eleven in the posse.

When they reached the cabin, the temporary tenants were long gone, but the trail was easy to follow because of the heavy rain the day before. They followed the Salt Creek road until, about thirty or forty miles north of Casper, around present-day Midwest, they ran afoul of the band, concealed behind a ridge known as Pine Bluffs. Shots were exchanged. No man was hurt, but three horses were hit and one was killed—and the robbers got away.

One of the shots spooked Sheriff Hiestand's horse, which raced off. The unlucky sheriff walked several long miles before finding another mount. But that horse, tired and work-worn, was so inadequate that Hiestand was forced to return to Casper, arriving about the same time as two posses from Laramie and other assorted officials, some on a special train. This group decided to remain in town to direct movements and await reports.

The posse in the field decided to play it safe, wait for supplies to catch up to them, and continue their pursuit in the morning. They did find the outlaws' campsite, which yielded some food and a Pacific Express gun taken in the robbery.

The next morning Hazen and his men continued their pursuit and once again came upon the robbers. Hazen and Casper physician John F. Leeper were in the lead, scouting hoofprints up Bothwell Draw just southwest of what is now Midwest, when suddenly gunfire rang out. Sheriff Hazen threw up his arms and fell from his horse, shot through the stomach, mortally wounded.

When Dr. Leeper tried to attend to him, he was also fired upon repeatedly for about ten minutes. Dr. Leeper fell down and played dead. As soon as the firing ceased, he did what he could for Hazen, but it wasn't much. Hazen hung on, barely.

In the heat of battle, the robbers had let their horses stray, so they were forced to escape on foot, wading into Casper Creek below their hilly stronghold. It was then about ten o'clock in the morning.

Pointer's history quotes from the unpublished manuscript, *The Bandit Invincible: The Story of Butch Cassidy*, arguably written by Cassidy as William Phillips, in the third person: "They missed judged the speed of the posse and was faced with each other, and the battle was on. There was 20 men in the posse to 6 of the Bandits. [These numbers don't agree with newspaper accounts.] Cassidy began by dropping the horses of the posse after they had fired on them. Kid Curry killed the sheriff. When the leader was killed the rest of the posse loaded the sheriff on a horse and was on their way to Douglas and the hold up was a success. The loot was $48,000. They went back to the big whole Canyon after a while to settle down to normal life." Cassidy was undoubtedly referring to the Hole-in-the-Wall country, his stronghold in Johnson County.

Somehow the posse found a wagon in which to bring Hazen back to Casper. The *Natrona County Tribune* of June 8 reported: "Genuine sorrow was depicted on the faces of our residents when it was learned that Hazen had been wounded. Crowds of people were on the streets awaiting the arrival of the wagon. It was intended to have him taken to the Natrona House, there to receive medical treatment…but he [Hazen] preferred to be taken to his house in Douglas if at all possible." Hazen's wish was granted, and he was taken there by special train where he died early Tuesday morning, June 6.

Joe Hazen was a well-liked man, forty-five years old, who left a wife and two small boys. Harry Drago's *Road Agents and Train Robbers* states, "Hazen was a very popular sheriff—a friend of the little fellers and not a tool of the powerful Wyoming Stockgrowers' Association as many sheriffs were." It was noted in the *Derrick* that his funeral in Douglas on June 8 was "one of the largest and most universally attended" ever held in the state. A special train was commissioned in Casper to take mourners to the funeral.

In Douglas, Hazen's friends lost no time gathering a posse. They brought their horses to Casper by train and joined the chase sometime around midnight of the same day that Hazen died.

About this time the *Wyoming Derrick* cryptically reported that one of the Natrona County officials had abandoned the pursuit of the outlaws. The writer hoped that there were mitigating circumstances for his conduct and concluded: "Friends and all alike criticize this apparent shirking of evident dangerous duty and if there are any valid reasons the *Derrick* will be glad to give them for the honor of the country." The alleged coward was not named and nothing more enlightening was ever published.

THE FAMOUS "HOLE IN THE WALL" CABIN

This 1914 photograph of a Hole-in-the-Wall cabin is from the Frances Seely Webb collection. The initials on the photograph could well mean that Webb got this photo from Jess A. Sheffner who was sheriff of Natrona County and a marshal of Casper from 1907-1914. (Frances Seely Webb Collection: courtesy Casper College Library)

For the next several weeks, one might say that pandemonium reigned throughout the countryside. Posses arrived in Casper from all over Wyoming—Rawlins, Glenrock, Douglas, Laramie—and raced away in all directions. Reports had the robbers showing up everywhere, all at the same time. A full company of state militia from Buffalo was scurrying around the Hole-in-the-Wall country. A United States marshal, Frank Hadsell, joined a large posse headed by Frank Wheeling, a Union Pacific special agent, galloping around the Big Horn Mountains and surrounding area. The well-known and respected Joe LeFors wrote in his autobiography, *Wyoming Peace Officer,* that he joined the hunt briefly at the request of the Burlington Railroad. LeFors, because of his vast experience and knowledge of the countryside, probably came closer to capturing the outlaws than any of the others. The robbers were still on foot, as they had been since their run-in with the Casper posse. With Marshal Hadsell and five other experienced men, LeFors nearly managed to run the robbers to ground—except for the bumbling interference of special agent Wheeling, who was averse to taking advice from anyone. LeFors was convinced that former Fremont County sheriff Arthur Sparhawk deliberately misinformed Wheeling that the outlaws' trail led to the Wind River Canyon. LeFors told Wheeling that none of the trails led in that direction, but Wheeling insisted, and their efforts were thwarted. LeFors felt, and probably rightly so, that in that part of the country, robbers had more friends than lawmen. LeFors was further critical of the Casper posse for not immediately surrounding the bandits after they shot Sheriff Hazen. Tired and disgusted after much maneuvering and little cooperation, LeFors quit the chase, rode into Casper, and left for Cheyenne to report to the Union Pacific superintendent.

J. Elmer Brock, an early pioneer whose family's home ranch lay near the north end of EK Mountain gives a firsthand account of the pursuit in that vicinity in his memoir, *Powder River Country.* Just sixteen years old at the time, he recounted that the robbers, on foot, went along Middle Fork and Red Fork to the top of EK Mountain trying to throw off their pursuers—men who he thought were all deputy U.S. marshals or deputy sheriffs. About sixty of them stayed at the ranch eating so much food that the ranch people existed on only one meal a day—if they could find anything left over. Brock mentions that Joe LeFors and Tom Horn were two of the officers.

Brock told about a futile attempt to capture the band supposedly entrenched atop EK Mountain. He himself had gone up the slope to round up saddle horses, but saw no one since, in his opinion, the robbers (whom Brock says he knew personally) had already slipped away. The posses surrounded the mountain on all sides and up they went. But they flushed out nothing except an "old silver tip bear" who scared the wits out of the men by charging around in the timber until it managed to break through the posse's line.

Brock wrote that there were just three robbers in the vicinity of his place, and he had no idea where the other three were. His recollection was that their loot amounted to "some sixty thousand dollars…a lot of jewelry, watches and some silver money." He identified the three outlaws on EK Mountain as George Curry, Kid Curry, and Harry Longabaugh. Brock rather admired George Curry. He knew him well because Curry had stayed at their ranch often and he considered him quite a gentleman.

Brock ended his tale this way: "Nothing…[at the home ranch]…was ever molested or stolen until the bunch of officers occupied the place…some of the officers stole a lot of blankets. Isn't it strange that as many outlaws as had been in that place that the first people to commit petty larceny should be a bunch of United States Marshals?"

By June 15, the robbery lacked one day of being two weeks old, the rewards had reached a total of eighteen thousand dollars, and the bandits were still eluding their pursuers. Drastic action was called for, so three trained bloodhounds were brought into Casper by train from Beatrice, Nebraska, and conveyed to the Tisdale Ranch on Powder River, near Kaycee, where they were put on the trail.

By this time the *Derrick* had described the three robbers in detail: "One man about 32 years of age; height, five feet, nine inches; weight, 185 pounds; complexion, light; eyes, light blue; peculiar nose, flattened at bridge and heavy at point; round, full, red face; bald forehead; walks slightly stooping; when last seen wore No. 8 cow-boy boots."

"Two men look like brothers, complexion, hair and eyes, very dark; larger one, age about 30; height, five feet, five inches; weight, 145 pounds; may have slight growth of whiskers; smaller one, age about 28; height, five feet, seven inches; weight 135 pounds; sometimes wears mustache."

The bloodhounds didn't have any better luck than their human counterparts. The June 22 issue of the *Wyoming Derrick* reported that the dogs' trainer, W.A. Johnston, returned to Casper by stage with one of the hounds the previous day, but the other two hounds were lost in the badlands, forty miles from Thermopolis—and it was hoped that they would eventually be found.

A 1902 *Century Magazine* quoted Dr. J.B. Fulton, who owned and trained the dogs, as saying that the bloodhounds had run down two of the robbers after a thirty-six hour chase. However, the cornered men protested their innocence. The lawmen, who had ridiculed the use of hounds, let the robbers go, whereupon, the dog handlers packed up and took the dogs back to Nebraska. Later, according to the article, after it was learned that "beyond the possibility of a doubt that the two men were implicated in the robbery," the lawmen acknowledged their error, and the dogs were vindicated.

The posse members laid the blame squarely on the shoulders of special agent Wheeling for allowing the robbers to escape. "He may be," the story said, "alright in the capacity of a 'spotter' on the UP" but he was definitely out of his element as a manhunter.

Now hopes began to dim. A week later the *Wyoming Derrick* carried the headline, "CHASE AFTER ROBBERS ABANDONED." The eleven-man posse headed by Special Agent Wheeling and U.S. Marshal Hadsell had lost the track on Kirby Creek in the Big Horn Canyon after following a false trail. They were finally ordered by dispatch to return to Casper, which they did—arriving on Friday night, June 23. They had ridden over a thousand miles. The paper "regretted that the authorities have deemed it best to discontinue the chase after the Union Pacific train robbers as these men should by no means be allowed to remain at large. It is not probable, however, that either the Union Pacific railroad company or the American Express company have abandoned all efforts to capture these men, but it is likely that they are going about it in a different way. This the *Derrick* believes is a wise course, and brave men who know the country thoroughly can do much more alone than by traveling in posses, especially when they keep three and four days behind the men they are pursuing." A swipe at agent Wheeling?

From this time on, the fervor of the chase and the passion of the press—and of just about everyone else in Casper—faded, dying a slow and lingering death, as the people of the community went about their everyday lives. A much later article in the *Derrick* on March 8, 1900, explained: "The most skillful manhunters in the country were employed, but the excitement died down to the slow, systematic work of the detectives which has ended in partial success." They were undoubtedly referring to the work undertaken by the Pinkerton detectives beginning in the latter part of July 1899 after the posses' failures.

Intermittent newspaper articles speculated on the rumored whereabouts of the robbers. An August 24, 1899, headline in the *Derrick* proclaimed that Currie and the Roberts brothers were reported to be in Chadron, Nebraska. George Currie's family did, indeed, live in Chadron.

On October 19 the paper reported that two men, whose true names were Bud Nolan and Dave Putney, were arrested as suspects. They had said their names were Tom and George Roberts, but evidence presented during their hearing established their true identities. They were unsavory characters, to be sure, but no concrete evidence linked them to the robbery, so they were let go.

On October 26 the *Derrick* reported the train robbers were captured—again—in Ogden, Utah. Not true. And again on November 30 an article emanating from Seattle purported to have one of the robbers in jail there.

At last on March 8, 1900, the *Derrick's* banner headline had the goods, proclaiming, "WILCOX TRAIN ROBBERS CAPTURED."

Bob Curry, alias Bob Lee, was captured while gambling at Cripple Creek [Colorado] and Louie or "Lonie" Curry was killed while attempting to make his escape from the officers in Missouri. It is claimed that these men, with an accomplice, were the men who, after riding through Casper, killed Sheriff Joe Hazen, and afterwards made their escape. This, in the opinion of those best in a position to know is a mistake, and while it is not only possible but probable that they are a part of the gang that held up the Union Pacific train last June, it is also almost certain that the three robbers who made their escape in this direction was George Currie and the Roberts brothers. It should be noted that the Curry killed in Missouri while resisting capture and the Curry arrested in Cripple Creek are not of the George Currie family.

The first two men belong to a family in Northern Montana, while the people of the latter live at Chadron, Nebraska.

In his history, Mokler expands the information on the three train robbers he says rode through Casper at two A.M. that Sunday. First was George "Flat Nose" Currie who was later killed at Thompson, Utah, by a Sheriff Tyler, whose posse was hunting local cattle rustlers, whose number included Currie. A telegram about this shooting was sent to Sheriff Hiestand in Casper on April 19, 1900. Pointer's book, however, gives a slightly different version, saying that the sheriff was hunting a local rustler and actually mistook Currie for the other man when Currie returned the posse's fire.

The second man Mokler identified as Harve Logan, alias Kid Curry, who, after another train robbery in July 1901, ended up in Knoxville, Tennessee, where he tried to pass a stolen fifty-dollar bank note and was captured after a breakneck chase. He was tried in Knoxville in November and was convicted on many criminal counts, but made a daring escape from the Knoxville jail. A few months later he was seen on foot in Kaycee "by a man who knew him well." Logan was trailed to a ranch on Bridger Creek belonging to Walt Puteney (though Mokler spells it Putney), where he was shot by the officers tracking him. But Logan's luck held: his companion got him onto a horse and they both escaped into the hills.

The third man was "one of the Roberts boys" whom Mokler identifies as either Tom or George Dickson, alias Tom or George Jones, alias one of the Roberts brothers. However, Pointer's *In Search of Butch Cassidy* carries a description of the Roberts brothers that approximates the physical characteristics of Harvey Logan and his brother Lonie—and those descriptions are very similar to the descriptions given in the *Derrick*.

Bob Lee's membership in the Wilcox train-robbery gang was never actually proven, but the Pinkerton agents finally ran him down in Cripple Creek. He was tried at Cheyenne on May 25, 1900, convicted and sentenced to ten years at the penitentiary in Rawlins. When released in 1907, he returned to Missouri.

Cassidy left Wyoming for Los Angeles, then met the Sundance Kid and Kid Curry in Albuquerque to discuss their plans. After several days, they moved on to San Antonio for the winter.

Pointer also recounts the fates of Elzy Lay and Ben Kilpatrick. Lay was tagged as one of a gang who staged a train robbery in New Mexico in July 1899. A posse captured him the next month; he was convicted and sentenced to life in the New Mexico penitentiary at Santa Fe on October 10, 1900, but was pardoned after serving five years. Eventually Lay returned to Wyoming where he got married and lived in both Baggs and Shoshoni. He then disappeared for several years, resurfacing in California where he died in 1934.

Ben Kilpatrick successfully pursued his outlaw career until, in St. Louis, he tried to pass some unsigned bank notes that had been stolen in another train robbery in Montana. He was arrested, convicted, and sentenced to fifteen years in the federal penitentiary in Atlanta in 1901. Released in 1911, he and an accomplice tried to rob a train in Texas the next year. The messenger in the express car attacked Kilpatrick, who had turned his back for a moment, crushing his skull with an ice mallet.

◈ ◈ ◈

The many and varied sources for this story make it—like the Wilcox train robbers—very difficult to run to ground. The conflicting versions of who, what, and how are natural, really, because there was such chaos at the time and so many people were involved.

The many men who were associated with and who rode with Butch Cassidy and his Wild Bunch all admired the charismatic, intelligent and commanding "social bandit" and they were extremely loyal to him.

Butch Cassidy was born Robert LeRoy Parker on April 13, 1866, which made him thirty-three years old at the time of the Wilcox robbery. He stood about five feet ten inches, with sandy hair and a complexion to match. A natural leader, he was good-looking, mostly good-natured, friendly, and well-liked. Throughout his years as Wyoming's most famous outlaw, he used a number of different names and was going by William T. Phillips, according to some accounts, when he died at Spokane, Washington, in 1937, at seventy-one years of age. Of course, other accounts report him dying in San Vicente, Bolivia, in 1909.

William Ellsworth "Elzy" Lay, was born November 25, 1868. He was twenty-seven years old when he joined up with Cassidy in 1895 and thirty-one years old at the time of the robbery. At five-eleven, he was tall, dark, and handsome, as they say, a quiet man, an expert gunman, and horseman. He took an alias, the name of William McGinnis, a boyhood friend, at some time during his outlaw career. Cassidy/Phillips called him "Harvey Gratwick" when he wrote about him. (Cassidy also called the Sundance Kid by that name in his writing.)

The Sundance Kid's real name was Harry Longabaugh. Born in 1867, he and Cassidy were close in age as well as build, but the Kid was darker complected than Cassidy, and a snazzy dresser. Usually quiet and reserved, he had a hair-trigger temper and was a crack shot. He and Cassidy were both champions of the underdog. Cassidy called him "Dick Maxwell" as well as "Harvey Gratwick" when writing about him.

Henry Wilbur "Bub" Weeks was also about the same age and size as Butch Cassidy, but much darker. He knew and worked with Butch around Cokeville, Wyoming, before joining his group.

Cassidy went to the Hole-in-the-Wall to recruit four more of his men—Currie, Logan, Odell, and Kilpatrick.

George "Flat Nose" Currie was born March 20, 1871, and his nose was his most distinguishing feature. He had a pleasant disposition and was well liked as a loyal friend.

Kid Curry's real name was Harvey Logan. Short, thin, and dark, he was thought to be part Indian. He was not at all friendly, and it didn't take much to make him mad. He was fearless and a ruthless, cold-blooded killer. Kid and his three brothers, Henry, John, and Lonie, were often referred to as the Curry boys. Henry, the oldest, died of pneumonia about 1885, and John, the youngest, was killed, so the only two Curry boys left were Harvey, about thirty years old, and Lonie, about twenty-six when they joined Cassidy. Lonie and Harvey looked much alike and both of them evidently had very prominent buck teeth. (The Roberts brothers whom Mokler said were the train robbers could very probably have been the Logans, according to Pointer.)

At over six feet tall, Ben Kilpatrick, whose name was often spelled Killpatrick, was nicknamed the "Tall Texan." This big, soft-spoken outlaw was, from most accounts, also dark and handsome like Elzy Lay. His most distinctive facial feature was a disfigured iris in his left eye.

The man called Dusty Bill Conner Odell seems to have no concrete identity and, according to Pointer, could have been any one of several different men.

The robbery and the resulting chase by the posses occupied the papers of Casper continually during the month of June 1899, then tapered off dramatically when no outlaws were captured. The last article of note appeared in the *Derrick* in June 1902. Thus the sand had drained from the hourglass.

CHAPTER SEVEN

ÇASPER'S
FIRST LYNCHING

FIVE MEN WERE incarcerated under the eye of William Charles Ricker, the popular and well-liked sheriff of Casper and Natrona County in December 1901—a winter that saw another landmark in Casper's criminal history.

The jail was then located on David Street, a block west of Center Street. Two of the inmates were brothers named Charles and Clarence Woodard, and neither was exactly an upright, law-abiding citizen by anyone's standards. Clarence, the younger, had spent nearly three years in the territorial prison at Laramie and had also served time in the Rawlins penitentiary. Charles, twenty-eight years old, was at least a part-time member of Butch Cassidy's Wild Bunch—as was Clarence.

According to Larry Pointer's *In Search of Butch Cassidy,* Charles Woodard was one of Cassidy's gang for the Belle Fourche, South Dakota, bank robbery on June 28, 1897. "Young Woodard" (then twenty-four), as he is referred to in Cassidy's supposed autobiography, *The Bandit Invincible,* was the fellow who held the horses during the holdup. The gang escaped, returned to Big Horn Canyon and divided thirty thousand dollars five ways, after which Charles was sent into Billings to see what was being said and written about the robbery—as well as to get supplies.

Three years later, Charles Woodard was again an eager and willing participant in another Wild Bunch escapade: the Union

Pacific train robbery at Tipton, Wyoming, west of Rawlins, on August 9, 1900. And once again Charles was the man in charge of the horses, taking them, according to Cassidy's account, about a mile west of the Tipton station where he was to build a small fire which would visually lead the rest of the gang back to their horses. This tactic was very similar to the getaway plan for the Wilcox holdup, though Woodard was not (so far as any recorded accounts go) a part of that caper. The Tipton robbery netted the Wild Bunch something like forty-five thousand dollars— more or less. (Estimates ranged from a mere fifty-four dollars to fifty-four thousand.)

The chain of events that led to the tragedies of both Sheriff Charley Ricker and Charles Woodard began in late November 1901. Charles Woodard, his wife Bertha, Clarence, and another brother, Harry, all lived in a comfortable cabin at the foot of Garfield Peak, the highest peak in the Rattlesnake Range, in what was called Garfield Park, about fifty-five miles southwest of Casper. They lived about five miles from their neighbors, Mr. and Mrs. Sam Hanes. The Haneses had gone away somewhere, and on that November day Charles, Bertha, and Clarence allegedly broke into the home and robbed them of almost everything there, including clothing, bedding, and food valued at three to four hundred dollars.

The angry Sam Hanes promptly swore out a complaint and Sheriff Ricker went after the Woodards, bringing Charles and Bertha back to Casper. Ricker's deputy, Ed Cameron, chased after brother Clarence and caught up to him about seventy miles north of Thermopolis. The two brothers were bound over to the district court on three-hundred-dollar bonds and lodged in jail on November 26. Bertha was dismissed.

By Monday evening, December 30, the Woodard brothers had been in jail a month, awaiting their trial on the charge of grand larceny in the company of three other prisoners. Those five would soon make their mark on Wyoming history. District

Sheriff Charles Ricker. Casper's first lynching occurred as a result of Woodard's murder of Ricker. (Mokler Historical Collection: courtesy Casper College Library)

court was due to convene in January, and Charles and Clarence definitely weren't planning to be a part of the agenda.

According to the *Wyoming Derrick* of January 2, 1902, one of the brothers had managed to steal a case knife at some time during their incarceration. The knife, the *Derrick* reported, was given to them along with the bread served to them in the jail. Using the knife, the brothers made a saw and, with painstaking effort, carefully sawed out the bars on a window on the north side of the jail, which left an opening about a foot square. Later conflicting testimony at the trial credited Bertha Woodard with supplying a saw to her husband.

When the brothers invited the three other prisoners to join the jailbreak that cold December night, two of them accepted the invitation. One was F.D. (Frank) Foote, described as a "no good bum" who had been charged with robbing a sheep camp, and the other was Thomas J. (Jeff) Franklin, accused of horse stealing. The third man, James Adams, also an accused horse thief, declined to go along, deciding, evidently, to take his chances on the mercy of the court. (Apparently he had also decided that he was too big to get through the foot-square opening.) Later trial testimony revealed that prisoner Adams had a girlfriend in Casper who allegedly gave a gun to Bertha Woodard who hid it in a prearranged spot where Charles could get to it after the jailbreak.

Prisoner Adams also told later that the men had worked at sawing through the bars for several days and had been finished for a week, but wouldn't leave because of the severe weather. There had been a snowstorm. The four others had also quarreled with Adams, hitting him and threatening to tie and gag him until he had promised not to say a word until they were well away. Adams confirmed that the men had stashed what food they could save from their prison meals for several days.

The opening in the jail window was so small that the four men had to take off their clothes, throw them out the opening along with a sack of food, and then squeeze themselves through, after which they dressed (around a corner of the building)—a pretty chilling maneuver. Prisoner Foote, a witty fellow, took time to write a brief message to Sheriff Ricker on the wall of the jail before he left. It said, "When this you see, remember me. For I a thousand miles will be."

The escapees ran west, nearly bowling over a little girl who was crossing the street behind the jail at the time—which was about 7:40 P.M. Then they headed south to the railroad tracks.

Emma Ricker, the sheriff's wife, who was alone with their children in their house abutting the jail, learned of the jailbreak from prisoner Adams within ten minutes. She gave the alarm by firing six shots from a revolver into the air: the standard call for help.

According to an account written by Frances Seely Webb and published in an annual edition of the *Casper Tribune-Herald,* Mrs. Ricker described Charles Woodard as a big man who must have had a terrible job squeezing himself through such a small opening. Fearing him, Mrs. Ricker spoke of him as being "like a tiger." She said Woodard's ambition was to be a "bad man." Woodard, it seems, courted a reputation as a dangerous gunman.

Sheriff Ricker and his deputies spent all night looking for the escapees, to no avail. At least three posses were organized and the telegraph wires sizzled as messages were sent everywhere, but the men remained at large.

Bertha Woodard, who was still in Casper, was promptly arrested again, but was released after two days when no one could prove concretely that she had anything to do with the jailbreak, even though she had visited Charles in jail just the evening before. She said later that she had never really expected to see her husband again.

On New Year's Day, Sheriff Ricker left Casper with a posse and headed west toward the Woodard place, intending to be gone for several days. The *Natrona County Tribune* reported that he and two of his deputies, James Milne and Clark Johnson, headed for the Woodards' cabin while the other two deputies were sent north. Ricker's posse arrived at the ranch at about five o'clock on the evening of January 2. The ranch was deserted except for a man named Jim Westfall and a Mrs. Sherman who made dinner for the posse.

While the men were eating, according to the eyewitness account of Milne—recorded in the *Derrick* on January 9—they heard a dog bark and saw a light in the stable and someone moving about among their stabled horses in the barn some thirty-five to sixty feet below the house.

The *Tribune* reported that the light in the stable came from someone striking matches and that Jim Westfall left the house and came back to say that the dogs were barking at coyotes.

The sheriff and his men had no way of knowing, of course, that Charles Woodard had found his way home and had sneaked into the barn. He got there by riding a horse that he stole from the Nicolaysen ranch pasture. Woodard realized immediately when he saw the horses in the barn that a posse was waiting for him. He was ready to make a run for freedom on one of the fresher horses belonging to the posse.

Inside the house, Sheriff Ricker decided—when the dogs refused to quit barking—to go down to the barn. His men earnestly advised him to stay in the house but he went anyway, saying, "I will go and see what is the matter myself." He thought that the third Woodard brother, Harry, who was nowhere to be seen, might be the man in the stable. Westfall agreed, telling Ricker that Harry was probably returning from McRae's sheep camp where he had gone early that morning on a business matter.

When Deputy Milne continued to object, Ricker said to him, "Oh, no, they wouldn't shoot me. I have always treated them well."

Ricker set off for the barn and was no more than ten feet from it when he was shot down. Deputies Milne and Johnson immediately fired on the barn for about thirty minutes. During this time they heard Sheriff Ricker beg for water and ask to be taken back to the house saying, "I would like to have a drink. I am dying. It will do no good to bring a doctor. Don't tell her." (Ricker was speaking of his wife.)

The deputies tried to persuade the shooter in the barn to let them come to the aid of their comrade, only to be refused with shouted oaths and threats.

Then the assassin dashed out, grabbed Ricker, and dragged him back into the barn where he beat him and stripped him of his watch, his money, and his left-handed six-shooter. Ricker died of a single bullet to the abdomen. He also sustained a one-and-a-half inch cut over his right eye, a cut through his upper lip, and a bruise on his chin. The postmortem declared he had probably died within half an hour.

Deputy Milne left the ranch on foot and plowed four miles over the mountains in waist-high snow to get to the nearest neighbor for a horse so he could ride to Casper for help.

Sometime during the night, Charles Woodard escaped from the barn taking two of the deputies' horses and a saddle. He was alone.

In Casper, the county commissioners and the prosecuting attorney met in special session and authorized a three-hundred-dollar reward each for the capture of the fugitives—dead or alive. More than thirty men were deputized to help, and the hunt for Charles and Clarence Woodard and the two other fugitives began with a vengeance.

All of Casper was devastated and enraged by the gruesome murder of their popular sheriff, whose funeral was held with much pomp and ceremony at the Odd Fellows Hall on Saturday, January 4. The funeral was reported to be Casper's largest service to date.

William Charles Ricker was sixty years old at the time of his death and would have had his sixty-first birthday on January 27. Born in London, he was the second of five children; he had three brothers and a sister. He and his family came to New York state from England when he was four years old. According to the *Derrick* he had been in Wyoming and on the frontier since 1884. An army scout and Indian fighter, he had been twice wounded in Indian battles—a shot in his hand had severed part of his little finger. He was married to the former Emma Odder in Laramie on May 2, 1885. They had four children, three girls aged sixteen, thirteen, and three, and a son aged eight, at the time of his death. Active in the Casper community, Ricker was Noble Grand of his Odd Fellows order. He was chief of the Casper Fire Department and a senior deacon of the Masons. Ricker had been sheriff of Casper for a year and had one more year to serve. He was buried in Highland Cemetery beneath a granite tombstone which reads simply, "W.C. Ricker, 1841–1902."

On January 6 three deputies who were keeping a very close watch on the Woodard place brought in two of the escapees, Jeff Franklin and Clarence Woodard. The bedraggled pair had made it to the ranch on foot and were hiding in the barn. They were unarmed and half starved, not having eaten much of anything for the better part of two days. After their capture, Jeff Franklin was interviewed by a *Derrick* reporter and told this story of the men's freedom flight.

> We all separated after getting outside the jail agreeing that we would meet three or four hours later at a point down the railroad track towards Glenrock and we all did come together down there about three miles from Casper except Foot [also spelled Foote] who left us immediately and would have nothing to do with us after we left the jail. All three of us, Charles Woodard, Clarence Woodard and myself all then started down the railroad track and during the night we went about twelve or fifteen miles then turning away from the track we came upon a deserted cabin where we stayed until Tuesday afternoon [December 31] at which time Charles Woodard left saying that he was going to Nebraska, that being the last we saw of him. Wednesday [January 1] we started in the direction of the Woodard ranch crossing the river below Casper. We reached the Twelve Mile reservoir Thursday afternoon where we laid out watching some parties moving a sheep camp. We were afoot and had been ever since we left the jail and had no guns with which to kill game so we were compelled to steal our food or go without which latter we did most of the time.
>
> From the Twelve Mile reservoir we walked to Oil Mountain which point we reached on Friday [January 3]

Charles F. Woodard, chained, and Sheriff Warren E. Tubbs at the jail. (Frances Seely Webb Collection: courtesy Casper College Library)

afternoon where we again ran into a sheep camp. Each night we laid out. Saturday we were pretty well on our way towards the Woodard ranch which we reached Sunday afternoon [January 5] where we ran into the officers. In going to the Woodard ranch we kept a good watch for tracks in the road and from what we saw we thought the posse with Sheriff Ricker had gone up in there but had come out again. The first we heard of the killing of the sheriff was when we were captured and for a time we believed the officers were joking for we thought Charles Woodard had gone east instead of west.

After the fugitives were brought to town, there was much talk of lynching them until it became established that they were not directly responsible for Ricker's murder. The threats of lynching Charles Woodard, however, did not diminish.

Charles and Clarence's other brother, Harry, was also arrested and brought to jail pending investigation. It was soon definitively proved that Harry was not at the ranch on the night of Ricker's murder. He had gone to Kenneth McRae's sheep camp four or five miles from the Woodard place and he slept there, not returning home until the next day. His story was later corroborated by Mrs. McRae.

It was on January 4 that Charles Woodard rode into a sheep camp on Powder River and told the herder, Tom McAffey, who knew him, that he had escaped from jail in Casper and was going to get out of the country. He cut off his mustache there and got McAffey to shave off his beard. After eating dinner and resting for a few hours, Charles rode off to the north.

According to later testimony (a letter from McAffey to the coroner's jury), Woodard told McAffey that he "had it in for" Ricker, his own brother Harry, and the Haneses. He had left the other escapees about eight miles below Casper and declared that he was not going back to jail. According to McAffey, Woodard was "very nervous, broke down and cried and said he had a little money." Woodard also had two revolvers with rubber handles— the left-handed one had been Ricker's—and a gunbelt full of .32-20 cartridges. He was wearing an old white hat, calfskin gloves, a black and yellow silk neckerchief and blue overalls.

From McAffey's sheep camp, Woodard's trail led up through Kaycee and Four Mile Gulch to Arvada. From there, his pursuers thought, he would either hop a Burlington freight train or go to the Crow reservation or into Montana proper.

At this time, Sheriff Neilson of Sheridan County offered a thousand-dollar reward for Woodard, so there were a good many people—including sheriffs—who were more than eager to apprehend the fugitive. Frank Webb, from Casper, was one of several men who trailed Woodard all the way to the Crow reservation in southern Montana, hoping, according to the *Derrick*, "to collect the reward for Mrs. Ricker." But they returned to Casper on January 27, having, unfortunately, lost Woodard's track after they entered the Crow reservation.

In the meantime, the *Derrick* reported that Deputy Sheriff James Kennedy had returned from the Garfield Peak country where he had recovered Sheriff Ricker's watch, papers, and six dollars in currency that had been scattered about the stable.

On the same day that Webb's disappointed party returned to Casper, the first big break in the case came about and, after that, events began to accelerate. Warren Tubbs, the new sheriff, received a telegram from Sheriff Hubbard in Billings: Charles Woodard had been captured, was in his custody, and Sheriff Tubbs should come for him immediately.

Tubbs left for Billings the very next day. The *Derrick* gave a detailed account of Woodard's capture. The later courtroom testimony of the two men who captured him, Wilson Owens and John Berkheimer, was somewhat different in detail.

The *Derrick* reported that Woodard arrived at Wilson Owens's ranch about thirteen miles west of Billings calling himself Bill Gad and telling that he had been in some trouble in Wyoming. A few days had passed until Owens happened to pick up a newspaper that carried an account of Ricker's murder and a very good description of Woodard. Owens and his hired man, Berkheimer, decided then and there to capture him. They sent to Billings for a pair of handcuffs and as soon as the handcuffs arrived, they went into action.

The three men were in the house talking on January 27 at about one P.M. when Gad/Woodard unbuckled and removed his two revolvers for the first time since he had arrived there. Owens and Berkheimer got between him and his guns and jumped him. They had a terrible fight, but they were finally able to subdue and handcuff their victim. According to the *Derrick* the two captors said Woodard begged them "piteously" to let him go so that he could run. They could then shoot him down "like a dog" and he wouldn't have to go back to Casper. He confessed to Ricker's murder, even telling them of the reward offered for him.

It was nearly midnight on February 1, when Sheriff Tubbs, the prisoner, and six deputies returned to Casper by train. The train was a good three hours late getting to town. The six deputies had boarded at Orin Junction earlier in the day as reinforcements just in case the rampant rumors circulating around Casper about "getting Woodard" had any substance. Casper's Mayor Cantlin had also prepared for any vigilante action by calling a special meeting of the fire department whose members placed themselves at the mayor's disposal.

Casper's reputation as a law-abiding community was at stake and the *Derrick* chastised the city's rabble-rousers, the Cheyenne newspaper, and the acting governor, Fenimore Chatterton, for feeding the rumor mills and for questioning that the town of Casper could act in a civilized and dignified manner. Chatterton had gone so far as ask Sheriff McDougal in Douglas to take charge of Woodard. "McDougal," the *Derrick* wrote, "flatly refused." The governor thought, further, that if Woodard couldn't be brought to Cheyenne for safety's sake, the state militia should be sent to Casper. Casperites were furious, and it was probably a good thing that the governor was way down there in Cheyenne.

When the train arrived in town sometime between eleven and midnight it could just as well have been high noon: at least three hundred people were waiting at the station. The officers actually had to help the trembling Woodard from the train, and the paper reported that the onlookers were shocked when they saw him. Mokler wrote in his *History of Natrona County,* "Woodard's head was cut open in three places, both eyes were blackened, and his face was bruised and cut in such a horrible manner that he could hardly be recognized by the people who knew him." Owens and Berkheimer had done a thorough job.

Mokler continued: "About thirty men formed a V at the steps of the passenger coach when the officers and the criminal emerged and they surrounded the three men and escorted them to the county jail, but the large crowd followed the party to the jail determined to lynch the murderer if they could get hold of him."

One of Casper's pioneers, W.S. Kimball, wrote a historical reminiscences column in the *Casper-Tribune Herald* in the forties called "Ye Good Old Days." His column of February 4, 1945, recalled the Woodard drama which differs from the earlier *Derrick* writings in many details—including the spelling of Woodard, which Kimball consistently spells "Woodward." Of Woodard's arrival back in Casper after his capture, he writes: "The entire male population was at the depot to meet him. Without previous planning [we] lined up in two single columns extending from the depot towards the Adsit Hotel [north across Midwest Avenue from the depot] standing along the outer edges of the sidewalk, facing in. Not a word was said, nor any demonstration made as acting Sheriff Tubbs marched his prisoner up the center of the walk between the two lines of men and to jail."

The *Derrick* reported that Woodard was hustled through the crowd which was quiet and orderly except for a little boy—who should have been home in bed—who hollered, "Hang him!" According to the *Natrona County Tribune*, Woodard remarked, "This a big reception ain't it?" He was soon closed into a steel cage at the jail, on David Street.

Jail security was very tight and Woodard, according to the *Derrick,* feeling that he was more or less safe for a while, began to relax and enjoy the notoriety. He shaved, he trimmed his fingernails, he sang, he smoked—all in good humor and all under close supervision. But he absolutely refused to talk to reporters. The *Derrick* reported that when he was searched at the jail, a small bucksaw was found sewn into a pleat of his shirt. Woodard reportedly said it was the very saw he had used on the prison bars a month earlier.

Franklin and Adams were still being held at the jail. Apparently Woodard talked to them—this according to the *Natrona County Tribune*—and admitted that he'd gotten his man (Ricker) anyhow. He said he would have gotten another if he hadn't been afraid that his friend at the house might get in the line of fire (possibly referring to Jim Westfall). Woodard also declared his hatred for Sam Hanes and his wish to do away with him, too.

District Court of the Second Judicial District convened on Wednesday morning, February 5, for the arraignments of both Woodard and his fellow jailbreaker, J. F. Franklin. Judge C.W. Bramel asked Woodard, who was handcuffed and chained, to answer the charge of murder, but Woodard asked, instead, for a court-appointed lawyer, declaring himself to be destitute. Judge Bramel said he would see to it, and Woodard was taken back to jail until the next day.

Franklin's trial commenced and it was a short one. He was convicted by ten o'clock that very night and sentenced to three years in the penitentiary for horse stealing. (Foote, the "no good bum" and poet prisoner, had disappeared successfully, and Clarence Woodard had not, at this time, been charged.)

Thursday morning Charles Woodard appeared again for arraignment this time with his court-appointed attorney, C. de Bennet. (De Bennet apparently had conversed earlier with Woodard in the jail and had declined taking his case, but the judge appointed him anyway.) De Bennet was soon joined by another lawyer by the name of John M. Hench.

Woodard pled not guilty, and his trial was set for the following Tuesday, February 11.

Woodard's lawyers filed an affidavit with the court asking for a change of venue, having obtained testimony from at least a dozen prominent Casper citizens swearing that Charles

Woodard could, in no way, be tried fairly in Casper. Judge Bramel refused their pleas, whereupon Woodard's lawyers asked for a week's continuance in order to round up some defense witnesses. The court agreed and the trial was postponed until February 18.

Meanwhile, a petition to Judge Bramel had been circulated around Casper by Frank Webb and three other men asking that a special prosecutor, Casper attorney Fred D. Hammond, be assigned to the case. Evidently Webb and company doubted the capability of the present county prosecutor, Alex T. Butler, for the simple reason that he had, so far at least, refused to let anyone else assist him in preparing the case against Woodard. The petition also questioned Butler's legal knowledge in general: "We most respectfully submit the present county and prosecuting attorney of Natrona County, Wyoming has not got the requisite ability to properly prosecute said case without error to a final determination." The petition was signed, wrote the *Derrick,* by about 175 citizens, only six citizens refusing to sign.

Prosecutor Butler's objection to an assistant prosecutor was, apparently, that one should not be appointed unless one could be paid. Matters were somehow resolved and attorney Hammond ultimately joined prosecutor Butler. (Butler subsequently brought action for libel against the signers of the offensive petition as well as the editor of the *Derrick* who editorialized that Butler was "crazy" as well as being a "fool.")

The trial began and jurors were chosen surprisingly quickly, although the entire original panel was dismissed due to preformed opinions. Thirty more potential jurors were called, and the jury panel was complete within a day.

The trial was held in the town hall which then stood on the west side of Center Street about midway between Second and First Streets. The *Derrick* observed that "the convening of court Wednesday afternoon [February 19] showed probably for the first time during the trial the great interest which the people of this town and vicinity are taking in the trial. Seats were taken in every available place and standing room was at a premium. A large number of ladies also were present, many being personal friends of Mrs. Emma Ricker....

"The defendant, Chas. F. Woodard, while consulting with his attorneys and taking an interest in the defense of the case showed apparently but little concern or nervousness as to the outcome of this, one of the most noted cases in the history of our county, if not in the entire west."

Before the trial got under way, Woodard's wife Bertha, along with his sister, were ushered out of court due to the possibility that Bertha, especially, might be called as a defense witness.

The two prime prosecution witnesses were John Berkheimer, who was put on the stand first, followed by his employer, Wilson Owens.

Berkheimer testified, the *Derrick* reported, that as Owens's employee he had met Charles Woodard at a hotel in Laurel, Montana, where Woodard was looking for work, and Owens agreed to give him a job. "Woodard," Berkheimer testified, "told me he broke jail in Wyoming having sawed out of jail and picked up an old pony and rode out to his place and when he got there they had some saddle horses in his barn and were laying for him. The sheriff came down to the barn and said, 'Is that you Harry?' He said he answered no and then shot him. He took Ricker's gun from him and beat him up. Said he shot the sheriff with a .38 caliber gun."

Berkheimer could not identify the gun, but he did identify the scabbard and continued his testimony.

He and Owens had planned to capture Woodard at dinner time. Woodard had taken off his guns, leaving them on a bed. Owens slipped Berkheimer the .45 and aimed the other gun at Woodard, who jumped up. Berkheimer then hit him on the side of the head with the .45. Woodard started to attack him and Berkheimer struck him again on the top of the head, knocking him down. As Woodard scooted partially under the bed Owens and Berkheimer managed to get the handcuffs on one arm, but Woodard grabbed a hammer lying at hand and hit Berkheimer on the nose. Berkheimer told him over and over to give up or he would kill him. The two men finally managed to subdue Woodard and handcuff his other arm. Berkheimer concluded his testimony by quoting their exchange of words.

Woodard allegedly said, "Boys, what is the matter?"

Owens replied, "You know what is the matter," and proceeded to read the description and account of the murder from the newspaper.

Woodard then said, "I took that gun off the son of a bitch that I killed." The gun, of course, was Ricker's left-handed piece that Woodard had evidently traded to Owens. The gun was then positively identified as Ricker's.

Owens was next called to testify and gave the following account, which was printed in the *Wyoming Derrick* on February 27.

First met Chas. F. Woodard at Laurel, Montana in a saloon. Woodard wanted some place to work or rest up. Woodard had his two guns with him, but the belts and scabbards were cached with his coat under the depot platform. He worked for me for some time under the name of Bill Gad. I showed Woodard the article offering a reward for his arrest and he said, "you see where I am at." Later that day he said he hadn't been treated right in Casper regarding bonds and that he killed Ricker at his ranch. Woodard said that while the things claimed by Sam Hanes were being loaded into the wagon he got his rifle and would have killed Hanes and his wife and Sheriff Ricker had it not been for his [Woodard's] wife. After breaking jail and on reaching his ranch he found three saddle horses in the stable and sheriff Ricker came down and said, 'Is that you Harry?' Woodard said he answered no and then shot him and left him kicking around on the ground and he

This photograph shows the Casper courthouse and the sheriff's quarters around 1910. The jail was located behind the residence and is not visible. The buildings were in a square block by themselves—David Street on the left, and Ash Street on the right. (Frances Seely Webb Collection: courtesy Casper College Library)

then hit him over the head. Woodard said he then lengthened out the stirrups of one of the saddles and turned out some horses and then rode away.

Woodard said that he knew he had one friend [Westfall] at his house the night he shot Ricker and would have shot the others could he have distinguished them. Woodard said that one of the inmates in the jail at Casper did not escape with the rest of them but he had a girl in Casper who got a gun and gave it to Woodard's wife who cached it so Woodard could get it. He stated that his wife gave him the saw which he used in cutting his way out of jail.

The case for the defense commenced on Friday afternoon, February 21 at about 4:00 P.M. The *Derrick* reported that the town hall was filled with even more people than had attended

This period watercolor by Bessie Jameson shows the sheriff's quarters with the attached jail to the rear. (Frances Seely Webb Collection: courtesy Casper College Library)

the famous McRae trial. Woodard's wife and sister were up front in the makeshift courtroom, but when Woodard tried to take hold of Bertha's hand, he was restrained by one of the officers who constantly watched him.

Defense attorney Hench announced that it was Woodard's desire to testify on his own behalf, though the defense counsels were opposed to that strategy. There were no other defense witnesses, and Charles Francis Woodard pretty well cooked his own goose, good and proper, with the story he related.

With tears in his eyes and a tremble in his voice, he told about his jailbreak, attempting to justify it by saying that his wife was being badly treated by his brother Harry and by the woman Harry had employed at the house—who must have been Mrs. Sherman.

He told about finding a revolver—the murder weapon—at the stockyards below town, but wouldn't say how it got there or who put it there.

He told how he hid at a ranch about six miles below town the second night and how he spent the next day in a coal bank nearby.

He told how he stole a horse from the Nicolaysens' pasture in the late afternoon and got to his ranch about dark.

He told about entering his barn, seeing the horses, and realizing that the posse was waiting for him.

He told about grabbing one of the posse's horses, mounting it, and then hearing Sheriff Ricker call, "Harry, is that you?"

He told about their dialogue. Woodard called back, "No, it is not Harry."

Ricker replied, "Oh, oh is that Charlie? Throw up your hands."

Woodard continued, saying, "I pulled my own gun then and said, 'Stand back' swung it around and said, 'Go back,' and it went off."

Now Woodard protested before the court that he in no way intended to kill the sheriff. He just wanted to scare him so Ricker would retreat to the house and give him a chance to get away.

> When I fired the shot he [Ricker] said, 'Oh' right out loud that way. I jumped off my horse and went back into the barn and did not hear anything for ten minutes and then Ricker came to and called out, 'Oh boys come and get me.' He called this way two or three times. Someone stood near the house for I could hear them talking. I thought they were coming to the barn and I held a gun and shot it off in the air so they would not come and get me. The men at the house then fired several shots.
>
> I went into the barn and laid down by the manger, the fellows [were] at the house all the time. One of them called out, 'You had better surrender for we have you surrounded.'
>
> Finally the sheriff called out, and these were the last words he spoke.

CASPER
WYOMING
~1905

This illustration of Casper, Wyoming, in 1905 was drawn for the Troy Laundry Company who used it on their calendars. The viewpoint is looking toward the southeast across the North Platte River. North Center Street starts near the words "Casper Wyoming–1905" and continues south toward Casper Mountain. The intersection of Center and Second is at the four largest flat-topped buildings. The street running parallel with the river is Yellowstone and the railroad follows present-day Collins Avenue. The jail, the attached sheriff's quarters, and the courhouse are in a block by themselves with David on their left and Ash on their right. (Frances Seely Webb Collection: courtesy Casper College Library)

It was at this point that Woodard began to sob. After he got himself under control, he continued:

> The sheriff said, "Won't you come and carry me to the house. Oh my poor wife and babies." He said this two or three times. I did not object to the men at the house coming and getting Ricker and had a good notion to just give up everything. It sounded so pitiful for the sheriff who was calling for his wife and babies, but I thought they would come and kill me so I saddled the horse, tied a long rope to the bridle, threw it out of the door as far as I could, then crawled out of a window and getting hold of the end of the rope went back into the barn and gave the horse a spat and by pulling on the rope brought the horse around to the window where I got on him and escaped. I knew the sheriff was dead when I rode away but I did not steal his money. His gun was lying on the ground and I picked it up and then unbuckled his belt and scabbard and put them on myself.

Woodard continued his testimony by telling of his flight across the country, his meeting with Owens and Berkheimer and his capture and unmerciful beating at their hands, despite his pleas to "Hold up. God Almighty, men, don't kill me."

He concluded his testimony by swearing that he didn't drag Ricker into the barn or strike or shoot him after he fell.

The evening session of the trial was to be devoted to the arguments of the lawyers. The paper noted that even more people had crowded into the town hall—if that were possible.

Prosecutor Butler took about ten minutes to sum up his case, after which defense counsel Hench probably surprised everyone considerably when he waived any argument for the defense. This ploy effectively prevented prosecutor Hammond from presenting a closing argument for the prosecution. Judge Bramel gave his instructions to the jury, and they began deliberating at about nine that evening.

An hour later the jury sent word that they were ready to render a verdict, but it was past eleven o'clock by the time Judge Bramel reconvened the court, since the crucial participants had to be rounded up. Woodard had been asleep in his cell at the jail and Defense Attorney de Bennet had gone home.

The spectators, though, had remained right in the courtroom, although many of the ladies had disappeared.

The paper noted that all the men who stayed were stern-faced and were known to be organized—with a leader—to carry out their own version of justice if the verdict was anything other than guilty. They needn't have worried.

Woodard was found guilty and was taken back to jail where, the *Derrick* reported, "the doomed man broke down and sobbed like a baby." He had himself under control by morning, however, and at that time said he felt "as good as could be expected under the circumstances."

At ten that morning, February 24, Judge Bramel sentenced Woodard—after a lengthy and impassioned discourse— "to be taken hence to the county jail of this county and therein confined under proper guard as provided by law until the 28th day of March, 1902 at which time between the hours of 9 A.M. and 3 P.M. you are to be taken to an enclosure specially prepared within the jail yard of said county and that at said time and place you be hanged by your neck until you are dead. And that God whose laws you have broken and before whose tribunal you must then appear have mercy on your soul."

The *Casper Tribune Herald* in its sixty-fourth annual history edition of March 28, 1982, featured a 1937 report of the Woodard case—an article asserted to be "Heretofore Unpublished Oddities and Phases of Interest in Connection With the Case." The article indicated no author and spelled Woodard's name "Woodward" throughout.

The most interesting variation in this article is the claim that Judge Bramel was somewhat inebriated at the time he was to sentence Woodard. The account claims that Judge Bramel, a dignified and competent jurist, was so overcome by the horror and tragedy of the case that he broke down sobbing and had to hand his typewritten sentence to the Clerk of Court to be read while "those who were close to him could plainly hear the liquor gurgle in a flask which the court had concealed in his inside pocket."

This statement is not borne out in any of the newspaper accounts, Mokler's history, nor in the reminiscence by W.S. Kimball who writes that he was the jury foreman. However, Kimball also spelled Woodard's name with the extra *w*, which could be a clue to the 1937 report's primary source. None of the other sources report that anyone other than Bramel read the sentence.

Woodard heard the sentence stoically, although a number of the courtroom spectators, both men and women, wept. On the way back to jail he laughed sarcastically about the "fair and impartial trial which people here say I have had." He asked a reporter not to "roast" him in print. He nearly broke down at the jail, however, when he asked Sheriff Tubbs if he could see his wife. The paper did not relate whether his request was granted, but reported that Bertha Woodard left Casper Wednesday (February 26, presumably) for Thermopolis where she intended to make her home.

A suspect presence permeated the Woodard-Ricker tragedy who was never really investigated properly and that presence was Jim Westfall. He was obviously a friend and associate of Charles Woodard. Many unsubstantiated rumors circulated indicating that it was Westfall who supplied Woodard with the murder weapon—or at least with access to it. Adding suspicion was Deputy Clark Johnson's testimony about Westfall's roamings on the fateful night at the ranch and about a private conversation between Westfall and Ricker outside the ranch house before Ricker was murdered. In addition, Woodard's own remarks concerning his "friend" should have raised a red flag, but didn't seem to.

The *Natrona County Tribune* had carried a story during the trial, on February 20, under a headline that declared, "The Defense Will Claim That Westfall Did It." The article said, in part, "The state's witnesses have sworn that Westfall shot from the house toward some object near the barn door and it will be claimed that this object was Sheriff Ricker, and it was Westfall who killed the sheriff instead of Woodard."

The defense counsels, of course, did no such thing. Why didn't they examine the part Westfall may have played in Ricker's death or what Westfall might have done to abet Woodard? Perhaps they felt the effort to do so was totally futile in the face of all the damaging testimony already given. Perhaps they were afraid: the general feeling in Casper must have been murderous and overwhelmingly in favor of a hanging. It's probably safe to say that few people were ready to listen to any other explanations by this time.

However deep Westfall's involvement might have been, he was never called upon to testify or explain his actions in any way. (He had been placed in custody in January while the coroner's jury investigated his supposed connection to the jailbreak, but finding no concrete evidence of involvement on his part, they had released him.)

On March 25, three days before Woodard's scheduled hanging, a nine-word telegram to the *Derrick* from its Cheyenne correspondent read as follows: "Supreme Court noon today granted stay execution Woodard indefinitely."

Woodard's attorney, C. de Bennet, had been in Cheyenne for days working to that end. Now the execution would likely be delayed for at least 105 days so that the Wyoming Supreme Court could review the case and rule on his application for a new trial.

In the meantime, the hanging scaffold had been erected on the north side of the jail. Sixteen feet high, it was enclosed by a high fence which was "securely braced on the inside to resist the pressure of a crowd," in the words of the *Derrick*.

The gallows, constructed next to the jail in the courthouse yard, awaited the arrival of the condemned man, Charles Woodard. From left: Park C. Hays, Sam W. Conwell, E. F. Seaver, unidentified, A. J. Mokler, Warren E. Tubbs (sheriff), and P.C. Nicolaysen. (Mokler Historical Collection: courtesy Casper College Library)

After the news of the stay of execution became known, a number of men, according to the *Derrick*, were set to gather in town "in order to be here on the day set for the execution" which was not only March 28, but also Good Friday. Casper's Catholic priest, Father Bryant, the *Derrick* reported, who had frequently visited Woodard in jail, disapproved of a hanging on such a holy day, and was happy to hear of the stay of execution. Though the good Father agreed that Woodard's sentence was just, he also claimed that, historically, no criminal had ever been executed on the day that marked Christ's death. Father Bryant's views didn't receive much support.

At about a quarter past midnight in the snow and darkness of that Good Friday morning, twenty-four well-organized and masked men came together to carry out Woodard's original sentence. As they rode toward Casper, they encountered Dr. E. P. Rohrbaugh on his way by horseback from Casper to deliver a baby at Bates Hole. The masked vigilantes stopped him and were prepared to hold him, but one of the party believed the doctor's story and they let him go on his way. The next morning as he was riding back to town, Rohrbaugh saw all the hoofprints in the snow leading to many of the ranches along the way. When he learned of Woodard's lynching, he realized who the masked men were and what they had done, Frances Seely Webb related in *Casper's First Homes*.

The masked vigilantes rode straight to the jail and knocked on the door. When Sheriff Tubbs, who had been asleep in his room, called out, "Who is it?" a voice answered, "The marshal."

Tubbs opened the door and the armed vigilantes, guns trained, jumped him, wrestled him to the floor, tied him up, gagged him, and threw him into his room, leaving two of their number to guard him.

Having removed the jail keys from Tubbs's pocket, the men went directly to the barred door leading to the prison corridor and Woodard's cell.

A jail attendant by the name of Erben was stationed on the other side of the barred door and found himself looking at a phalanx of masked and armed men whose guns were pointed right at him. Making a snap decision that discretion was the better part of valor, he let them through the door.

The *Derrick* in its extra edition reported that Woodard didn't resist the men but did try to put on his clothes because he was wearing only a flannel shirt. Someone said, "Never mind your clothes, you won't freeze to death."

The *Derrick's* gruesome account of the next minutes was undoubtedly a firsthand one because it related that two newspapermen, having heard the lynch rumors, had decided to check things out shortly after midnight. They were prowling around the prison where all seemed quiet when suddenly a figure, followed by others, came out of the jail's door. The reporters, "scenting a mystery," climbed the fence and made for the doorway where "more than a score of men stood…masked to the eyes while a few others led the doomed man through the alleyway into the courtyard."

As the reporters approached within ten feet of the men, someone cried, "Halt. Hold up your hands, you are not wanted here," and the revolvers were aimed at them.

The reporters identified themselves and the armed men then told them they could stay, but they were not to interfere—and they were to accurately report what was happening.

Five of the masked men took Woodard up on the scaffold and quickly fixed the noose around his neck. The group fell quiet and Woodard said, "Let them put all this in the newspapers."

Then he spoke again. "Tell my darling little wife that my last words were for her." He seemed perfectly in control of himself and "asked his executioners to make the noose a little longer."

The reporters' account concluded:

All was ready for the springing of the trap but none of the men seemingly understood the mechanism. There were several minutes delay during which the doomed man spoke. "Good-by everybody, may the Lord have mercy on my soul. Boys make it a little longer than that. Just a little. Don't choke me boys" was added in a conversational tone to those with him on the scaffold. "Let me tell you once more before I die that I never shot Ricker purposely. Good-by. God have mercy on me and you boys."

These were the last words of the doomed wretch as being unable to spring the trap, several strong arms seized the half nude body and cast it over the rail surrounding the scaffold. Then ensued a most horrible sight. On the rope coming to full tension every muscle in the suspended man's body was convulsed while a horrible choking sound emerged from his throat. For some moments this continued when recognizing that the impetus had been insufficient two of the masked men sprang forward…exerting all their strength on the wretched man's legs…for some minutes…

until there was no more movement. Then one of the masked men stepped up to Woodard's body and pinned to his flannel shirt a piece of paper that read, "NOTICE process of law is a trifle slow. So this is the way we have to go. Murderers and thieves beware."

Someone said, "Scatter!" The masked vigilantes then swiftly and silently left the enclosed stockade. The reporters watched as the men dispersed in all directions.

Alfred J. Mokler, who owned, edited, and reported for the *Natrona County Tribune,* was one of the reporters who witnessed the hanging that night and wrote about it in his autobiography years later. He related that this hanging was the first and only one he had ever seen and he never wanted to see another. His paper also put out an extra edition of more than twelve hundred copies—which kept him up all night—but there were many other sleepless nights for him, he wrote, when he was assailed by memories of "the contortions and writhing of the body" and "the sickening, groaning, gurgling sound that came from his lips as he was being strangled to death."

Mokler said that he personally knew all the men who comprised the group of vigilantes, and he wondered how they were able to live with themselves in view of the way he, himself, felt as a mere spectator. Only one of the vigilantes ever talked to him about the hanging, and he apparently had no regrets whatever.

Mr. Mokler said that many of the vigilante group had died, at the time of his writing, some of them tragically; some had experienced business failures while others "have become physical and moral wrecks." He, and others, speculated that perhaps these men were being punished by God despite the fact that Woodard deserved a hanging—a legal hanging.

The Woodard capture, reward, trial, and construction of the gallows cost the Natrona County taxpayers at least four thousand dollars, according to figures in the March 6, 1902, *Wyoming Derrick*. Considering the sparse population and the value of a dollar at the time, this was quite expensive. Some thought it money wasted, considering the outcome. The *Derrick* opined, however, that it was money well spent, as good and sufficient proof that Natrona County citizens weren't going to stand for such lawless goings-on.

Charles Francis Woodard, twenty-eight years old, was buried in an unmarked grave at Highland Cemetery. Today, still unmarked, it is surrounded by the imposing monuments and vaults of a number of prominent Casperites who might have objected quite strenuously had they known the company they would keep...or maybe not.

CHAPTER EIGHT

TIED TO THE TRACKS

"IT WAS A DARK AND stormy night" when a drama to equal the *Perils of Pauline* occurred in Casper. And who knows? Maybe the *Pauline* storytellers were inspired to tie *her* to the railroad tracks after hearing about the desperate plight of Adolph Kuhrtz, whose bizarre adventure took place in Casper on an autumn night in 1911, a night that seemed to suit the crime dramatically—dark, cold, and stormy.

The thirty-five-year-old Kuhrtz was working the evening swing shift at the Midwest Oil Company refinery which years later became the Amoco refinery. In 1911 the refinery stood about a mile from town, and it would be years, yet, before Casper grew westward far enough to surround it.

At about ten o'clock on Saturday night, November 11, Kuhrtz, a relatively new employee of the refinery, was in the boiler room shoveling coal into the boiler. (His duties also included being the night watchman—an ironic circumstance considering the impending drama.) As Kuhrtz shoveled—a noisy task—two men wearing caps and masks which completely covered their faces entered the boiler room by the door behind Kuhrtz. Kuhrtz didn't hear or see them until they were "almost upon him," according to the story in the *Natrona County Tribune*. Startled, he turned to face them and one of the men asked him, "Are you the fireman here?"

The Tribune *newspaper office, 1898. It stood on the east side of South Center Street across the alley from the back of the present Rialto Theater, about halfway between East Second and East First Streets.* (Mokler Historical Collection: courtesy Casper College Library)

Kuhrtz said that he was. The same fellow then said to him, "Do you expect to hold your job here right along?"

Kuhrtz replied, "Yes, the company has hired me and I think I will stay with them."

"Do you work all night?" was the next question.

"Yes," Kuhrtz said. Actually, Kuhrtz was due to be relieved at midnight.

"Well, you won't be here in the morning," one of the men proclaimed. Kuhrtz noticed that the men took pains to disguise their voices and "changed their manner of speech several times."

Both men then jumped on the hapless Kuhrtz, tied his hands with a rope, and shoved under his nose a cloth or sponge which had likely been saturated with ether or chloroform. Kuhrtz immediately began to feel very drowsy, but before he passed out he heard one of his captors say, "We'll carry him over to the tracks."

The tracks he referred to were the Chicago and North-western Railroad tracks which paralleled the southern boundary of the oil company property.

When Kuhrtz regained consciousness, he was tightly bound across the railroad tracks. His neck was tied to one rail, his feet to the other, and his arms and wrists were also securely bound. Kuhrtz had no idea how long he'd been unconscious. He was lying face up and he was very, very cold.

For two hours Adolph Kuhrtz lay across the "frosty steel rails" suffering the agonizing cold and surely besieged by frantic thoughts. Would he die here—cut to ribbons by a freight train whose engineer would never see him in time...would he never see his wife and children again...how could this happen to him...who hated him enough to leave him to this cruel fate? The rope that bound his crossed wrists was half an inch thick, but he managed to work and twist his hands until the rope was loose enough to free them. By this time, however, his hands were so cold and numb that they were virtually useless. He couldn't use them to free himself from the ropes wound around his body, under his armpits, and around his feet which lay across the parallel rail.

At midnight Kuhrtz's relief, Horace Evans, arrived at the refinery. Evans looked at the water level in the boiler and saw that it was very low, something that was not supposed to happen. A little uneasy, Evans began to wonder what had gone wrong. It occurred to him that Kuhrtz might have had an accident somewhere on the plant—or that he might even have fallen into the open water well.

Evans found a lantern and went outdoors to look around. The water well was only about two hundred yards from the railroad tracks, and, when Evans approached the well, he heard a faint groaning.

Kuhrtz, only barely conscious, did see and register the flickering lantern in the darkness. He tried to call to Evans, but he

was so cold and weak that his cries couldn't compete with the
frigid, howling wind.

Evans was a persistent man, though, and kept looking.
Within half an hour he had found Kuhrtz. By that time it was
about half past midnight and Kuhrtz had been tied to the tracks
for about two hours.

Evans untied Kuhrtz and helped him into the refinery building as quickly as he could. Then he telephoned a Casper doctor,
Homer Lathrop, asking him to come to the refinery right away
and to bring Sheriff Sheffner with him. The superintendent of
the refinery, William Detrich, was also called to the scene.

The men found poor Kuhrtz in pretty sad shape, and Dr.
Lathrop took him to the hospital in his car. It was feared that
Kuhrtz's hands and feet were so badly frozen that amputation
might be necessary. (Fortunately, that did not prove to be the
case, although he did lose his fingernails and one toenail.
According to the *Tribune* of November 15, 1911—which called
the attack "A Dastardly Deed"—the Midwest Oil Company
paid for Kuhrtz's hospital stay and saw to it that he had the very
best care available.)

Superintendent Detrich immediately notified the general
manager at the company's headquarters, asking him to appropriate five hundred dollars for a reward to encourage the apprehen-
sion and conviction of the criminals. The local company matched
the amount, bringing the reward total to one thousand dollars.
The very next day a man named Bennett was arrested on suspicion of the crime, but nothing came of it, and he was let go.

The motive for the "dastardly deed" remains a mystery to
this day. It wasn't a robbery: nothing was taken from Kuhrtz's
person—neither his money nor his watch—and nothing was
missing from the refinery. People speculated that, because of
some grievance or other, the criminals were planning to sabotage
or blow up the refinery, but there was no unrest at that time
among any of the refinery workers according to Superintendent

A fire truck drives down Center Street in what appears to be a parade.
(Sheffner-McFadden Collection: courtesy Casper College Library)

Detrich. One might wonder, however, whether it was a crime of envy, since Kuhrtz was such a new employee of the refinery. One of the masked men had asked such odd questions about his employment there. Might he have been an applicant for the job that Kuhrtz got, mad as hell that he didn't land the job himself?

Further speculation hinted that because Kuhrtz was not a member of the workers' union, some labor agitators had figured they would make a frightening example of him.

The *Tribune* offered no possible motive, noting that "Kuhrtz has a wife and two little children in the city. He has been in Casper for about a year and has always been an industrious and inoffensive fellow minding his own affairs, and interfering with no one. He drove the bakery wagon for the Wheeler and Skinner Company during the early spring and later waited table at the Edelweiss Restaurant, and he does not know that he has an enemy in the town." The paper went on to opine that if the two men who attacked Kuhrtz were captured, they would likely be snatched from the sheriff's clutches and executed without benefit of a trial.

Kuhrtz spent about two weeks in the hospital and was discharged near the end of November, fully recovered. He went right back to work at the refinery and remained an employee there until he retired on March 13, 1941, his sixty-fifth birthday. The Midwest Oil Company had, by then, evolved into the Standard Oil Company of Indiana.

The date of the attack on Adolph Kuhrtz is something to marvel at: November 11, 1911, becomes, in figures, 11/11/11. The actual attack on Adolph's person probably occurred at about eleven P.M., making this sequence; the eleventh year (1911), the eleventh month, the eleventh day, and the eleventh hour.

◈   ◈   ◈

The Kuhrtz family remained residents of Casper after retirement. Emma Kuhrtz died in Casper on April 22, 1961, at the age of seventy-eight.

Adolf Kuhrtz lived to a venerable ninety-one years of age and died on January 19, 1968. His obituary appeared the next day in the *Casper Star-Tribune* along with his picture which showed a nice-looking, bespeckled gentleman reading a copy of *U.S. News and World Report.* The notice said that he had come to Casper in 1913—an obvious error—and that he recalled that there were only three automobiles in town at that time. The article mentioned that Kuhrtz was an avid gardener and had been in the "merchandising business" back in Ellis Grove, Illinois, which was his home before he came to Casper and where he was married to his wife, Emma C. Dressel, on September 21, 1905.

Mr. Kuhrtz was survived by his children in Casper and a sister in Missouri. He was buried beside his wife in the family plot at Highland Cemetery.

The obituary made no mention of the "dastardly deed" which certainly proved that Adolph Kuhrtz was one of Casper's most unflappable citizens.

CHAPTER NINE

A TRAGIC TRIANGLE

GEORGE EDWARDS, AT thirty-four, was a prosperous rancher and sheepman whose spread lay on the south rim of the Bates Hole country some thirty to forty miles south and west of Casper in the area still referred to as Freeland. He was living there in 1911, with his wife and four children aged two, four, six and eight. Edwards had come to Wyoming from Kansas in 1897, married his wife in Rawlins in 1903, and was now an industrious and successful man, reputed to be worth forty to fifty thousand dollars, not an inconsiderable sum in those days.

It was in April of 1911 that a fellow showed up at the ranch looking for work—or a handout. The fellow said his name was Roy Landers. Edwards fed him supper, let him stay the night, and subsequently hired him on a temporary basis for a month, which turned out to be a terrible mistake.

Roy Landers, unknown to Edwards, was a convicted felon who used a couple of aliases when needed: Roy Grant and Grant Smith. About twenty-nine years old, he had been in trouble with the law at least since 1900. In today's terms he had been an eighteen-year-old teenaged juvenile delinquent—bigtime. His parents and family lived in Minatare, Nebraska, and, though he was born in Arizona, he lived most of his crime-filled life in Wyoming.

In 1900 he had been sent to the Rawlins penitentiary for two years from Sheridan County where he had been convicted of grand larceny. After he was released, he was caught in Uinta County for horse stealing and sentenced this time for two to four years. The *Natrona County Tribune* and the *Casper Record* reported that he was sentenced on April 16, 1910, but had soon after been pardoned from that sentence upon the pleas of his mother. He found his way to the Edwards ranch in April 1911.

After working a month or six weeks for Edwards, Landers quit and made his way back to Nebraska. During his short stay at the ranch, however, he managed to become well enough acquainted with Mrs. Edwards to begin writing to her frequently, urging her to leave home and join him in Nebraska.

About the middle of December Landers showed up unexpectedly at the Edwards ranch, and the family invited him to stay for a while and have Christmas dinner with them. Landers was still at the ranch in mid-January, Edwards testified, when the two of them started out for Casper one morning and were intercepted by a messenger on his way to the ranch with a telegram for Landers informing him of his mother's death in Nebraska. The messenger wanted ten dollars for bringing the telegram and, since Landers didn't have any money, Edwards paid.

When they got to Casper, Edwards gave Landers another twenty dollars, for whatever reason, and then picked up his mail. There he found a bill for twenty-four dollars, incurred by Landers when he had done a chore for Edwards in Medicine Bow.

Feeling, no doubt, considerably poorer—if not wiser— Edwards took Landers back to the ranch to work off his debt. Landers immediately "played off sick" and spent three or four days in the house with Mrs. Edwards where, Edwards learned later on, Landers threatened to kill his wife unless she agreed to run off with him.

Edwards next sent Landers out to herd sheep, but that didn't work out, either. The other herders complained that not only did Landers shirk his duties, he was actually killing off the stock by not feeding them and, further, he was making salacious remarks about the "neighborhood" women. The men said he also bragged that now that his mother was dead he was going to get her money. Landers also bragged about the women he'd led astray, the homes he had wrecked, the horses he had stolen, and the man he'd murdered in Montana. Apparently Landers had been twice married—his first wife divorced him while he was in prison and the second wife left him for another man in Saratoga who ultimately killed her. His co-workers found him intimidating and were afraid of him.

Edwards finally had enough and fired Landers whereupon Landers borrowed a horse from a fellow named Al Johnson and rode off to Shirley Basin where he had plenty to say about Mrs. Edwards. He boasted that he would persuade her to run away with him within six months even if he had to kill her husband and "knock the brats in the head." He bragged that he had broken up five other homes, and this effort would "make it one more."

Edwards later testified that during that spring his wife began to get dirty postcards from Landers. She became distraught, even suicidal, and begged her husband to help her; she began to have nightmares from which she woke up screaming.

Then, one day in July, Mrs. Edwards set off to Casper with two of the children and two of the hired hands, leaving her husband no explanation.

The next evening as Edwards—no doubt perturbed—was out cutting oats, one of the hands, Fred Ott, returned with the children, but no Mrs. Edwards. A note addressed to George from his vanished wife read, "Dear Husband: God bless you and the children. Take care of them. Don't tell nobody where I've gone."

The thunderstruck Edwards cared for the children that night. The next day he left the eight-year-old girl in charge of the younger three and rode over to Shirley Basin returning with his friends Bill and Kate West. The Wests took the children back to Shirley Basin, and Edwards spent the next five days—without eating or sleeping, he said—trying to decide what to do. He finally decided to go to Casper where he spilled the whole sordid story to Sheriff Sheffner.

The sheriff had no trouble tracking Landers down. From Minatare, Nebraska, he and Edwards trailed Landers to Lingle, Wyoming, where the sheriff apprehended him at the post office one morning as he was picking up his mail. They then found Mrs. Edwards about five miles out in the country where she had been living with Landers for the past month. She said that she stayed with Landers only because of his death threats to her and her whole family.

Edwards whisked his wife away to her sister in Lincoln, Illinois, staying there with her for a short while. Mrs. Edwards seemed to be suffering severe mental and emotional trauma but, nevertheless, Edwards soon returned to Casper. Within a week or so Mrs. Edwards also returned to Casper, the family was reunited, and they tried to make the best of a bad situation, according to Edwards.

In the meantime, Roy Landers was cooling his heels in the Casper jail and occupying his time with threats to kill the entire Edwards family as well as the sheriff, the deputy sheriff, the judge, and everybody who had anything at all to do with his capture or conviction.

Landers took great pleasure in bullying the other prisoners, hitting one of them over the head with a chair. He tried to make a saw using a table knife and parts of an alarm clock that he destroyed. Sheriff Sheffner pretty clearly had his hands full with his troublesome prisoner and finally made him wear a twenty pound "Oregon boot" day and night.

During his six months in the Casper jail, Landers was charged, pled guilty, and was convicted of enticing a female for the purpose of prostitution and stealing another man's wife away from her husband and children. That winter he was

Lights were officially turned on in Casper on June 12, 1900, but at first there were only four streetlights. This photograph, with prolific streetlights, was probably taken about ten years later. (Mokler Historical Collection: courtesy Casper College Library)

sentenced once again to the Rawlins penitentiary, this time for twelve to fifteen months. Edwards thought the court was much too lenient and that the sentence should have been more like fifteen *years*.

On Friday, January 24, 1913, George Edwards—who was, he testified, still haunted by the fear that Landers would somehow manage to murder him and his family—came to Casper having been summoned for jury duty for the following Monday. He had some business to take care of, he said, so he arrived in town early with the hogs he planned to sell.

It was then, Edwards alleged, that he learned that Landers had been convicted and sentenced. And it was then that Edwards made up his mind to kill Landers. He later testified, "I knew he would kill me when he got out and all of a sudden it came to my mind that if I had to be killed I would try and kill him first." (Sheriff Sheffner told a reporter for the *Casper Record* newspaper that when Edwards came to town there were rumors that there might be trouble.)

The next morning, January 25, Sheriff Sheffner and his brother Claude, who was also one of his deputies, gathered up Roy Landers and another prisoner named Wolford, chained them together, and started north up Center Street toward the railroad station and the journey to the Rawlins penitentiary. It was about 10:30 A.M. (Mokler's *History of Natrona County* gives January 26 as the date of the incident which disagrees with Sheffner's recorded testimony.)

Knowing that the sheriff and his prisoners were due to leave for Rawlins, Edwards had hidden his .32-20 Smith & Wesson revolver in his pocket. He was leaving Webel's general store, on the east side of Center Street between First and Second Streets, after doing some trading, when he saw the little procession of prisoners and lawmen—bucking a fierce wind—coming slowly along the street from the courthouse, which was a block to the north, behind them.

Stepping back into the recessed doorway of Webel's store, Edwards took his gun out of his pocket and waited. As the procession crossed the alley between the *Tribune* building and the store, he stepped out of the doorway, aimed for Landers's heart, and fired. The bullet hit Landers in the left breast and pierced his lung. Landers ran out into the street dragging Wolford with him. At 180 pounds, Landers was much larger than Wolford, who was also crippled; when Wolford fell down, so did Landers.

Sheriff Sheffner jumped ahead of the prisoners and grabbed Edwards's gun hand, telling him to "cut it out." Edwards was ready to shoot again, but the sheriff took the revolver away from him.

Edwards said, "That is all I want. I am now satisfied." Landers was lying in the street fully conscious. Someone asked him where he was hit and he said, "over the heart."

Casper doctors Lathrop and Leeper were both called, as was "Shortie" Castle who owned the livery stable. It was he who drove Landers the short distance to the doctors' private hospital—probably in his second-hand Reo automobile, the fourth car to travel the streets of Casper. (According to the paper, the doctors' private hospital was the former residence of Tom Spears, on South Durbin Street, which they had purchased from him and remodeled into their hospital.) Landers spent the journey cursing and threatening Castle, who had previously lodged a complaint accusing Landers of stealing one of his livery horses. Landers would have been prosecuted for that crime if his other crime had not been more serious.

Once at the hospital—indeed, while he was on the operating table—Landers also threatened to "get" Dr. Lathrop as soon as he got out of the penitentiary. Landers, however, did not get out of anywhere except this life. Edwards's bullet had severed a main artery, and he bled to death within the hour.

The sheriff notified Landers's family—his father and two brothers—and on the following Tuesday the father and one

A horse and rider put on a performance at the Grand Central Stables. Some say this is a stuffed horse, used to stage photographs. (Mokler Historical Collection: courtesy Casper College Library)

brother arrived in Casper, took possession of the body, and left the next day for Minatare where Landers was buried. He was thirty-one years old.

Despite the fact that the hastily called coroner's jury declared that Landers came to his death as a result of a gunshot wound inflicted by a party or parties unknown, Edwards was charged with first-degree murder. The district court was in session and the trial was scheduled for a mere nine days after Edwards's arraignment. The *Record* reported that just a week and two days had elapsed: a record for a murder trial, "being the quickest one ever tried in the United States."

The trial began on Monday, February 3. The courtroom overflowed with the curious—many from Bates Hole and many friends of Edwards. The jury was selected by one o'clock that afternoon. Starting at two o'clock, all the evidence was presented in a quick forty-minute session, whereupon the judge called a recess. The lawyers then held a conference with the judge over a point of law, and the proceedings were adjourned for the day.

The next morning, with the courtroom again overflowing, Edwards was called to the stand and, without being sworn in, told his story. After he had finished, three witnesses testified briefly that they had known the defendant for years and that he was a peaceful, law-abiding citizen. The judge then gave his instructions to the jury. At ten-thirty that morning the jury began deliberation. Two hours later they returned a verdict of not guilty which pleased everyone "in the county." Edwards was released, returning home by one o'clock in the afternoon.

Later reports in the *Casper Record* and the *Casper Press* testified that Edwards "had the sympathy and support of everyone" in Casper as well as the whole county and that in the following weeks and months "he and his wife became reconciled and were apparently living happily together."

The story might have ended, mercifully, here. However, early on Monday evening, June 9 (dates vary), the couple's supposed happiness came to a violent end when George Edwards, in a "jealous rage"—according to the *Casper Press*—"shot to death Fred Ott," one of the ranch hands who had accompanied Mrs. Edwards to Casper that fateful day a year before.

Perhaps because of the ease with which he was exonerated in the killing of Landers, Edwards may have thought that, once again, he could take matters into his own hands to protect his wife's person and reputation. In fact, he said later that he felt perfectly justified in this second killing.

Suspecting that she and Fred Ott were conducting an intimate affair, Edwards devised a plan to catch them in their supposed illicit liaison.

On the afternoon in question, Edwards told his wife and Ott to go to the neighboring White ranch, about four miles west, and borrow a sack of flour. He also told them that he was leaving for his sheep camp and wouldn't be home until the next day.

Mrs. Edwards gathered up her children and with Fred Ott started off for the White ranch in a white-topped buggy. It was about four o'clock in the afternoon.

As soon as the little party was well away from the ranch, Edwards, according to his own testimony, bored a hole in his kitchen floor, got his gun—the same Smith & Wesson he had used to kill Landers—and hid himself under the floor. He would use the peephole he made to spy on the unsuspecting couple when they returned from the White ranch.

It was about six o'clock when Mrs. Edwards, the children, and Fred Ott returned home. Ott brought the sack of flour into the house, emptied it into the flour bin, and then, according to Edwards's story, began teasing Mrs. Edwards by dusting flour onto her face and arms and telling her that she didn't need any flour "below"—that she was good enough just as she was.

Both Edwards and his wife later testified that she ordered Ott out of the house at that point, but that he refused to leave. (In contrast, the newspaper reports stated that Ott did go to the bunkhouse to wash up and then returned to the house.) It was then that Edwards crawled out from under the house and entered the kitchen shooting. His first shot went wild, lodging in a thermometer hanging on the wall.

Mrs. Edwards began screaming and ran from the house while Ott dodged toward the living room. Edwards kept shooting and pumped two or three more shots at the fleeing Ott, who fell to the floor.

Edwards turned and ran outdoors, chasing his wife. Ott made his way toward the bunkhouse about forty yards away, crossed the plank which spanned the irrigation ditch in between, and disappeared into the bunkhouse. Then he stood in the bunkhouse door and said, according to the *Casper Press,* "There is no need to send for the sheriff, send for a doctor and when I get well I will talk to you." He disappeared back inside.

It was evidently some time after this—and after Mrs. Edwards left for the White ranch, this time to summon help—that Edwards went into the bunkhouse and shot Fred Ott a final time.

Eliza White later testified that when Mrs. Edwards got to her place at about eight o'clock she was crying and, between sobs, related that her husband had shot Fred Ott. She asked Mrs. White to send her hired hand for the doctor and begged the woman to go home with her.

Mrs. White said that when they got back to the ranch the house was dark—it was about ten o'clock—and Mrs. Edwards wouldn't go in, so she knocked on the door herself. When no one answered, she and Mrs. Edwards began to tend to the wagon and the team of horses. Then a light came on in the house, and George Edwards came to the door and invited Mrs. White to come in. Apparently Mrs. Edwards stayed outside. Edwards was getting his clothes on, and he went into the children's bedroom where he had put the children to bed. Mrs. White followed him and said that Edwards was very excited and his eyes were "bulging out."

He said, "I suppose they will be after me again."

Mrs. White said, "Is Fred dead?"

Edwards said that he was. They left the children's bedroom and went into the dining room where Eliza asked him to give her his gun.

When Edwards asked her if she was afraid of him, she told him she was not but, in her later testimony, she revealed that she was, indeed, very much afraid.

Edwards said he'd left the gun on a chair in the bedroom, so Eliza found it and hid it under the mattress. When the sheriff arrived at the ranch the next morning, she retrieved the gun and gave it to him. Edwards told Eliza that it was the same gun he

This house was originally built about 1905-1907 by Mr. and Mrs. Thomas Cardinal Spears. Dr. Homer Lathrop leased it and remodeled it into a private hospital beginning in 1912. The home's address then was 840 S. Durbin; today's address is 938 S. Durbin. (Mokler Historical Collection: courtesy Casper College Library)

shot Landers with and, in practically the next breath, said, "Jimminy Christmas, I'm hungry."

Edwards was also quoted by his wife as saying that when he followed Ott into the bunkhouse "I plugged him again and didn't wait for him to die. I came away and went back and he was dead."

George Edwards apparently talked to Eliza White at length that Monday night—getting it all off his chest, so to speak. He told her that his wife's honor was the dearest thing in his life and that Ott confessed to his "intimacy" with Mrs. Edwards before the last fatal shot.

Sheriff Sheffner and Dr. Lathrop started for the ranch early the next morning after being notified of the shooting. Their car stalled, or ran out of gas, a couple of miles from the ranch and Edwards came out to meet them on horseback, telling them they were too late: Ott was dead.

Dr. Lathrop said to Edwards, "What's happened, George?"

Edwards replied, "The ___ __ _ ___ tried to mix in my family affairs again and I had to stop him."

Dr. Lathrop rode Edwards's horse the rest of the way to the ranch while Edwards walked.

The doctor and the sheriff stayed for two days at the ranch, conducting interviews and gathering evidence. That first morning Edwards and his wife had a private conversation (according to Eliza White's later testimony) after which Edwards told Eliza again of Fred Ott's "intimacy" with his wife; how Ott had been trying "to get the best of her"; how he'd gotten to him just in time.

Mrs. White said to Edwards, "How about the third [fatal] shot?"

Edwards replied, "We won't talk about that."

Mrs. Edwards said, "Will Mrs. White tell that?"

Edwards said, "Living over here she couldn't very well do anything else." (Edwards had apparently begun to realize the significance of his premeditated final shot, and he didn't want Mrs. White to say anything about it.)

Adding to the evidence of premeditation, the *Casper Record* reported that Edwards's seven-year-old daughter related "that after her mother went away Ott came to the door of the bunkhouse and stood there with his hands to his head and her father went down there and had another quarrel with him and shot him again."

The paper went on, "...if this part of the story proves to be correct Edwards will have less sympathy than ever for it would be hard to conceive a more cold-blooded deed than going out after some time had elapsed and finishing his already desperately wounded victim." The *Press* also stated that when Mrs. Edwards and the "other woman" (Mrs. White) arrived at the ranch and George Edwards told them that Fred Ott was dead, Mrs. Edwards tried to commit suicide by taking laudanum, but that she (Mrs. White) intervened. This bit of information, however, was not mentioned in Eliza White's testimony at Edwards's preliminary hearing.

The coroner's inquest was held at the Wood and Foshay "undertaking room." George Edwards was present but "unmoved" throughout the proceedings. The verdict was that Ott died from being shot by a gun in the hands of George Edwards.

The preliminary hearing was held on June 26 before Justice of the Peace Warren Tubbs, and that was when Eliza White gave her damaging testimony. She was the star witness and the courtroom was packed. Everyone wanted to hear her story. Mrs. Edwards, however, was most notably missing.

George Edwards was not represented by counsel and when he was asked to plead guilty or not guilty, he waived examination.

After Mrs. White's testimony—and that of the sheriff, the coroner, and the doctor—Justice Tubbs told Edwards that in accordance with the evidence presented, he was binding him over to district court for trial and that there would be no bail. He also advised Edwards not to talk to anyone without a lawyer.

Edwards requested, and was granted, a change of venue in the interest of fairness, so his trial was moved to the Converse County Court in Douglas.

On January 9, 1914, Edwards was found guilty of second-degree murder and was sentenced to serve not less than twenty or more than twenty-one years in the state penitentiary. The judge was C.E. Winter, and the popular opinion of his sentence was that Edwards got off lightly, indeed.

Mrs. Edwards and the four children were reported to be in attendance at the trial. Mokler's history states that as soon as the trial was over Mrs. Edwards took off her wedding ring and gave it to her husband, telling him that she was through with him. The *Casper Press* reported that she disappeared for parts unknown, deserting not only her husband, but her children as well.

Mrs. Edwards remains an unpredictable and elusive character throughout the newspaper reports and courtroom testimony.

She is never referred to by a first name, even though every other woman in the drama was accorded a given name. (Although all reports state that Edwards and wife were married in 1900 in Rawlins, the only marriage license on record there was issued to George Edwards and Lena Belle Baughan on August 11, 1903, so probably her given name was Lena Belle.)

◈　◈　◈

On February 6, two officers took Edwards and his four little children to Cheyenne where Edwards was lodged in the Laramie County jail. The officers and the children spent the night at the Plains Hotel.

The next morning the little party boarded the westbound Union Pacific train to Medicine Bow and Rawlins. The children disembarked at Medicine Bow where they were met by Mrs. Kate West, the same lady who took care of the children after their mother ran away with Roy Landers. She had evidently agreed to take care of them once again.

An article in the *Cheyenne Tribune* said of the children, "The Edwards children are attractive flaxen haired youngsters of happy and friendly dispositions. The greater part of their lives have been spent on a remote ranch and so delighted were they with the pleasure of travel and the sights of the city that they did not trouble about their predicament. Edwards, manifestly broken by his experience and worry over his future and that of his offspring, was very gentle to the children. Speaking of them he choked and with difficulty repressed tears.

"The present instance is believed to be the only one in Wyoming history in which children have accompanied their father on his way to the penitentiary."

According to Mokler, George Edwards was pardoned after several years in the penitentiary, and he relocated to southwest Wyoming with his children where he established a ranch and home.

◈　◈　◈

Conflicting or confused dates are frequently found in old newspapers and histories, but the Edwards saga seems to have more than its fair share.

As previously mentioned, Mokler's history says Edwards shot Landers down on Sunday, January 26, 1913, conflicting with the account in the *Casper Record* which claimed that the shooting happened "Saturday forenoon," January 25.

The date of Fred Ott's murder is all over the calendar in newspaper accounts, history books, and courtroom testimony— ranging from June 6 in one trial report in the *Casper Record* to June 17 in Mokler's history. However, research points to June 9, 1913, as the most logical date of the murder.

AFTERWORD

A MAN FOR ALL SEASONS

ONE MAN'S NAME APPEARS again and again in the early accounts of Casper.

Alex T. Butler was clearly a continuing presence—a mover and a shaker, if you will—in almost everything Casper. He was county attorney, newspaperman, gentleman rancher, and real estate entrepreneur. His name appears no less than twenty-three times in Mokler's *History of Natrona County* and probably twenty times that in the Casper newspapers spanning the years 1890–1911. One might say he was Casper's "man for all seasons" as his activities encompassed just about everything or anything going on in Casper.

Butler was a lawyer and as such a player in many of the cases of capital crime.

He successfully prosecuted John Conaway for the killing of Jack Tidwell in Lou Polk's dance hall. He was the prosecutor for the Hodge/Warren shooting case which he eventually lost, and for Hurt's trial which was also an eventual loss. As prosecuting attorney in the Woodard trial, he was accused by a few individuals of not knowing enough to prosecute Woodard; Butler later sued them. In the Woodard case, Butler was directed by Governor Fenimore Chatterton to identify the vigilantes who hanged Woodard and prosecute them for "debauching the state's fair name." He ignored the governor's directive because most

Elma Butler in her wedding dress at age sixteen in 1892. The picture was taken in Chicago where she and her new husband traveled shortly after their wedding so that attorney Butler could take care of some legal business with colleagues there. (Picture courtesy of Louise Butler Clark)

Alex Butler. (Frances Seely Webb Collection: courtesy Casper College Library)

everyone in Casper was firmly united in the opinion that Woodard got just what he deserved. Nothing more came of the request. Butler probably felt he'd had enough grief with this trial and enough was enough.

After the organization of Natrona County in April 1890, the county's second election of officials was held in September of that year. Alex T. Butler was nominated on the Republican ticket for county attorney. He lost to the Democratic candidate, but was later appointed to the office for the 1891–1892 term. He was next appointed to consecutive terms as county attorney in 1899–1900, 1901–1902, and for the last time in 1905–1906. (Butler's law library was assessed in 1890 to be worth one hundred dollars in contrast to that of his Democratic rival, Carl C. Wright's, assessed at fifty dollars.)

Butler first ventured into the publishing business when he bought Casper's first weekly newspaper, the *Casper Weekly*

Mail, in May 1890. His ownership didn't last long, however. The paper ceased publication in January 1891 while under Butler's ownership.

Not to be deterred, Butler jumped right back into the newspaper milieu when he leased the *Natrona Tribune* plant in June 1893 becoming publisher, managing editor, and probably writer, too. This time he persevered only two months before he hired W. E. Ellsworth to run the paper.

Next, Butler became the owner of the *Casper Press* in August 1908, serving as its editor, too, until January 1909 when H. J. Peterson took over the operation.

Both Butler and his wife Elma were prominent in the Natrona County Pioneer Association founded in Casper on November 12, 1901. Elma Butler was one of twenty-two charter members, and, at the association's first annual reunion the next November, Alex Butler and Governor DeForest Richards were among the dignitaries giving speeches to honor the occasion.

In social affairs, of course, he originated and carried out the renowned Columbus Club Balls. He was also the first Council Commander of the Woodmen of the World when it was organized in Casper in 1896 with thirty-one charter members.

As a real estate entrepreneur, Butler owned much land in and around Casper. In 1908 he sold five lots at Second and Wolcott Streets in partnership with Lucy Morrison Moore, his mother-in-law, for the proposed future post office. They received eleven thousand dollars for these lots. His own home, which also housed his law offices, stood on East Second Street, on the site of the recently closed Kline's dress shop. Today a residential area in southeast Casper in the vicinity of the Wyoming Medical Center carries his name. The building lots there at the Butler Addition were part of the original Butler homestead.

He had livestock interests as well, particularly sheep, which he probably acquired through his wife's family. (He had some lesser sheep interests with Joel Hurt at one time.) Butler's mother-in-law,

Elma Butler at age eighty-three on January 25, 1962. Mrs. Butler is sitting under a framed photograph of Casper in 1890. (Frances Seely Webb Collection: courtesy Casper College Library)

according to Webb's *Casper's First Homes*, was known in the early days as "Sheep Queen of Wyoming" and his wife Elma later acquired the title of "Sheep Queen of Natrona County." Elma actively operated their large sheep ranch.

Alex T. Butler died on September 8, 1911.

The *Casper Record* reported on the next day that citizens were "stunned" when "word got around" that Butler had died in Omaha. He had gone there with his son, Mifflin, where they sold a shipment of sheep. He was found dead in a bathtub at the Iler Grand Hotel in the small hours of Friday morning.

Mifflin recounted that at about midnight Thursday he was awakened by his father who asked him where to find the bathroom, after which Mifflin evidently went back to sleep. Later two "draymen" arrived at the hotel and, after checking in, wanted baths. The only bathroom available they found to be in use. The men heard water running and, after waiting around for an hour, reported that something must be wrong in there. Fortunately for the hotel anyway—the water was running all that time—Butler died before putting the stopper in the drain.

At an inquest in Omaha it was determined that Butler must have died from apoplexy.

This newspaper report is not accurate according to the Butlers' daughter, Louise Clark, who relates that Mifflin, fourteen years old, had gone to see a movie and when he returned to the hotel saw water running from under the bathroom door and down the hotel stairs. He opened the bathroom door and found his father, the victim of a heart attack.

Mifflin and his mother brought his body home to Casper on Sunday, September 10, and Butler's funeral was held the next day.

The *Record* noted that Butler was a Casper pioneer, had practiced law for over twenty years and was heavily invested in sheep and real estate. He was fifty-one years old.

According to the *Tribune* Butler was born in Rockford, Illinois, on February 20, 1860, and came to Douglas, Wyoming, in 1886, moving to Casper in 1889. He married Elma in 1892. Again, Mrs. Clark corrects the newspaper saying that her father was born in England, educated at Oxford, then emigrated to Rockford. From there he traveled to Bedford, Massachusetts, where he lived with a maiden aunt for a short time.

He took to heart the advice of Horace Greeley—"Go west young man"—and found his way to Casper, his destiny and the love of his life, according to his daughter, though the Butlers' marriage was not a long one.

Mrs. Butler remained in Casper for the rest of her life, living at 124 South Beech, according to Webb's book. Son Mifflin preceded his mother in death but is not buried in the family plot. Elma Butler was a venerable ninety-seven years old when she died in September 1974.

The Butlers' elaborate family burial plot at Highland Cemetery also contains the grave of a baby daughter, Lucy, who died in 1901 at the age of seven months. Louise Butler Clark, the only Butler child living, has been a life-long resident of Casper and relates that her mother sent to Vermont for the marble that became her father's tombstone.

Casper Magazine of December 1978 said this about the Butlers: "As a young man who was going places, Alex was strictly a city man, but Elma wasn't content to settle down as just a good wife. At her insistence they bought 'thousands of acres' on Elk Creek where she could fulfill her wishes to run her own sheep ranch."

It was undoubtedly these holdings that helped Elma Butler become something of a real estate mogul after she gave up actively running the sheep business.

The article continued that "around 1913" Elma made the decision "to go into the real estate business" and began "subdividing the old family homestead into what is now known as the Butler Addition, as well as a second addition located around where the hospital now stands. Then she bought a new Chalmers automobile to drive customers around and began her second career by selling lots. When she was ninety years old Elma was still selling lots and sitting at her typewriter taking care of the paper work."

Though Alex Butler may have been Casper's "man of all seasons" in his day, after his death his wife Elma picked up the family torch. Their daughter Louise Butler Clark, in her turn, continued the tradition as an astute Casper businesswoman and a vital link to the area's heritage.

BIBLIOGRAPHY

These sources, plus court and census records, were invaluable in the writing of this book. They are not a complete record of all the interesting and varied material that I found or stumbled upon by any means; but they are, nevertheless, the rock from which this volume sprung:

"Butch Cassidy and Other Wild Bunch Members Were Remembered by Lander Central Wyoming Pioneer E.J. Farlow," *Wyoming History News*, Volume 41, No. 8.

Casper Press. Issues spanning August 1908 through June 20, 1914.

Casper Record. Issues spanning April 1911 through June 17, 1913.

Casper Star-Tribune. January 20, 1968.

Casper Tribune Herald. April 6, 1968, and March 28, 1982.

Casper Zonta Club. *Casper Chronicles*, 3rd printing 1975. Articles and commentary by Story Committee comprised of: Irene C. Patterson, Garnett L. Dowling, Marguerite Bishop Minty, Frances Seely Webb, Edness Mokler, Edness Kimball Wilkins, Marjorie Hileman. Casper, WY: Mountain States Lithographing, 1964.

Cheyenne Sun. June 28, 1894.

Cheyenne Tribune. 1914.

Clark, Louise Butler. Interview by author. Casper, WY, February 5, 2000.

Drago, Harry Sinclair. *Road Agents and Train Robbers*, 2nd printing. New York: Dodd, Mead & Company, 1973.

Farlow, Edward J. *Wind River Adventures: My Life in Frontier Wyoming*. Glendo, WY: High Plains Press, 1998.

"The Fighting Shepherdess," *Casper Magazine*, Volume 2, No. 8, December 1978.

Hendry, Mary Helen. *Petticoats & Pistols*. Casper, WY: Mountain States Lithographing, 1992.

Horan, James D. & Sann, Paul. *Pictorial History of the Old West*. New York: Crown Publishers, Inc., 1954.

Le Fors, Joe. *Wyoming Peace Officer*. Laramie, WY: Laramie Printing Company, 1953.

Mokler, Alfred James. *History of Natrona County Wyoming*, Centennial Edition. Casper, WY: Mountain States Lithographing, 1989.

Natrona County Tribune. Issues spanning January 1897 through November 1911.

Natrona Tribune. Issues spanning June 17, 1891 through June 1897.

Patterson, Richard. *Wyoming's Outlaw Days*. Boulder, CO: Johnson Books, 1982.

Pointer, Larry. *In Search of Butch Cassidy*. Norman, OK: University of Oklahoma Press, 1977.

Randall, Art. *Casper "Old Town" and Fremont, Elkhorn and Missouri Valley Railroad*. (No publisher; no date).

Webb, Frances Seely. *Casper's First Homes*. Casper, WY: Mountain States Lithographing, 1978.

Wyoming Derrick. Issues spanning May (21) through June (5) 1902.

INDEX

CHARLOTTE BABCOCK is passionate about Wyoming history and obsessed with tracking down answers to mysteries, two necessary assets for a writer/researcher. As a Casper native, she has long been curious about its colorful past. *Shot Down!* is the result of years of personal interviews and research into Casper's frontier crime.

Babcock is an award-winning author, published in many genres including humor, children's stories, poetry, fiction and non-fiction. She has edited six books and is the author of one previous book. Her work has appeared frequently in collections, magazines, and newspapers.

She was honored as one of fifty exemplary alumni during Casper College's fiftieth anniversary festivities and is active in community affairs.

Her husband of fifty-one years, their two grown daughters, and four grandchildren are often the inspiration for her humorous writing.

*A special limited edition of 200 copies of this volume
was printed simultaneously with the trade paperback edition.
The special edition is Smythe sewn, bound in Patriot Red Kivar 7,
embossed with Skiver texture, and stamped in copper foil.
It is designed to be sold without a dust jacket.*

*The text is composed in
twelve point Adobe Garamond.
Display type is Ablefont Outlaw
with ornaments from Crop Circle Dingbats and Way Out West.
The book is printed on
Glatfelter Supple Opaque Natural
an acid-free, recycled paper
by Central Plains Book Manufacturing.*